THE SOUTHERN WORLD

THE SOUTHERN WORLD

Adapted from TO THE ENDS OF THE EARTH
by Irene M. Franck and David M. Brownstone

A Volume in the Trade and Travel Routes Series

Facts On File
New York • Oxford

THE SOUTHERN WORLD

Facts On File, Inc.
460 Park Avenue South
New York NY 10016
USA

Facts On File Limited
Collins Street
Oxford OX4 1XJ
United Kingdom

Library of Congress Cataloging-in-Publication Data

The Southern world: adapted from To the ends of the Earth by Irene M. Franck and David M. Brownstone.
p. cm.—(Trade and travel routes series)
Includes bibliographical references and index.
Summary: Describes the history of trade routes and commerce in the New World, including the Panama Route, the Inca Royal Road, the California Mission Trail, and the Cape Horn Route.
ISBN 0-8160-1881-2
1. Trade routes—America—History—Juvenile literature.
2. America—Commerce—History—Juvenile literature. [1. Trade routes—America—History. 2. America—Commerce—History.]
I. Franck. Irene M. To the ends of the earth. II. Series.
HE323.S68 1990
909'.09812—dc20 90-37446

A British CIP catalogue record for this book is available from the British Library.

Facts On File books are available at special discounts when purchased in bulk quantities for businesses, associations, institutions or sales promotions. Please contact the Special Sales Department of our New York office at 212/683-2244 (dial 800/322-8755 except in NY, AK, or HI) or in Oxford at 865/728399.

Jacket design by Catherine Hyman
Composition by Facts On File, Inc.
Manufactured by R. R. Donnelley & Sons Company
Printed in the United States of America

10 9 8 7 6 5 4 3 2 1

This book is printed on acid-free paper.

CONTENTS

LIST OF MAPS

PREFACE

The Southern World is one volume in the Travel and Trade Routes series. The series itself is based on our earlier work, *To the Ends of the Earth*, published by Facts On File, Inc., in 1984. This adaptation of the work for young readers has been prepared by Facts On File; many new illustrations have also been added. The maps, drawn from *To the Ends of the Earth*, are by Dale Adams.

Irene M. Franck
David M. Brownstone

INTRODUCTION

What Is a Trade Route?

In a world without airplanes, engine-powered ships, trucks, or even paved roads, how did people journey from one place to another? How did products that were found only in a very small part of the world eventually find their way across the continents? For almost 5,000 years, people have been bringing products from one part of the world to another using trade routes. Traders from Europe, Asia, and Africa carried furs, spices, silks, pottery, knives, stone utensils, jewels, and a host of other commodities, exchanging the products found in one area for those found in another.

When trading first began, there were no real roads. Local traders might follow trails or cross steep mountain passes in their treks from one village to another. With the passage of time, tracks were widened and eventually paved. The new paved roads tended to follow the old trade routes, thus establishing these routes as important links of communication between different cultures.

As technology advanced, sea-lanes became vital trade routes between the various continents and made possible trade with North America, South America, and Australia. Many of the highways and seaways that have been used predominantly for trade throughout history have shaped the course of events.

Why Study Trade Routes?

Studying the trade routes is one way of learning about the history of the world. As we look at the trade routes of Europe, for example, we can see how the nations of that continent have changed throughout the centuries: we learn how Scandinavian Vikings came to sail south and west, settling in France and Britain; we can appreciate how present-day Hungary was originally settled by a wandering tribe from the Ural Mountains. In a similar way, by looking at the trade routes of Africa, we can trace the history of the slave trade and learn about the European colonization of Africa in the 18th and 19th centuries.

In addition, studying the trade routes helps us better understand the origin of many of the institutions and services with which we are familiar today. Postal systems, tolls, guidebooks, roadside restaurants, and hotels all came into being, either directly or indirectly, because of trade routes. Studying the trade routes will help you understand how they emerged.

How to Use This Book

This book is organized in chapters. Each chapter is devoted to the history of one trade route, or in some cases, when the particular trade route has an especially long and eventful past, to a particular era in a trade route's history. Therefore, you can read about one trade route that particularly interests you or, alternatively, about all the trade routes in a given area. At the end of each chapter, you will find a list of books for further reading. This will assist you in locating additional sourcebooks should you need them to support report research or classroom work. If you are using these books as references for a particular history course, check the index of each to find the subject or person you need to know more about. All the maps are listed in the front of the book so you can find the location of each trade route.

Studying trade routes can be a fascinating way of learning about world history—and of understanding more about our lives today. We hope you enjoy all the volumes in the Travel and Trade Routes series.

1

THE PANAMA ROUTE

THE PANAMA ROUTE: CONNECTING EUROPE TO THE EAST

For centuries, people in Europe valued goods from Asia. Traders carried silks, spices, jewels, porcelain, cottons, and ornaments from India, China, and the Spice Islands, crossing the Middle East to reach the people of Europe. Some goods, like spices, did not grow anywhere but in the Far East. Other goods like fine porcelain "china," were luxury items desired by Europeans.

Until the end of the 15th century, Europeans were content to receive these goods from Eastern traders. Indian and Arabic sailors and merchants carried these goods along the Spice Route from Far Eastern ports via Africa or the Middle East and on to Europe. For hundreds of years the Europeans had little idea of the route these goods traveled or of how to go after those valuable products themselves.

Then, for many reasons, the Europeans decided to look for their own way to the East. Spanish, Italian, and Portuguese sailors took their ships eastward by various routes. One of the most important of these became the Panama Route.

Running into the Americas. One of the ways that Europeans tried to get to the East was by sailing west. The explorer Christopher Columbus reasoned that if the world were round as scientists were beginning to believe, he would reach India sooner or later by sailing

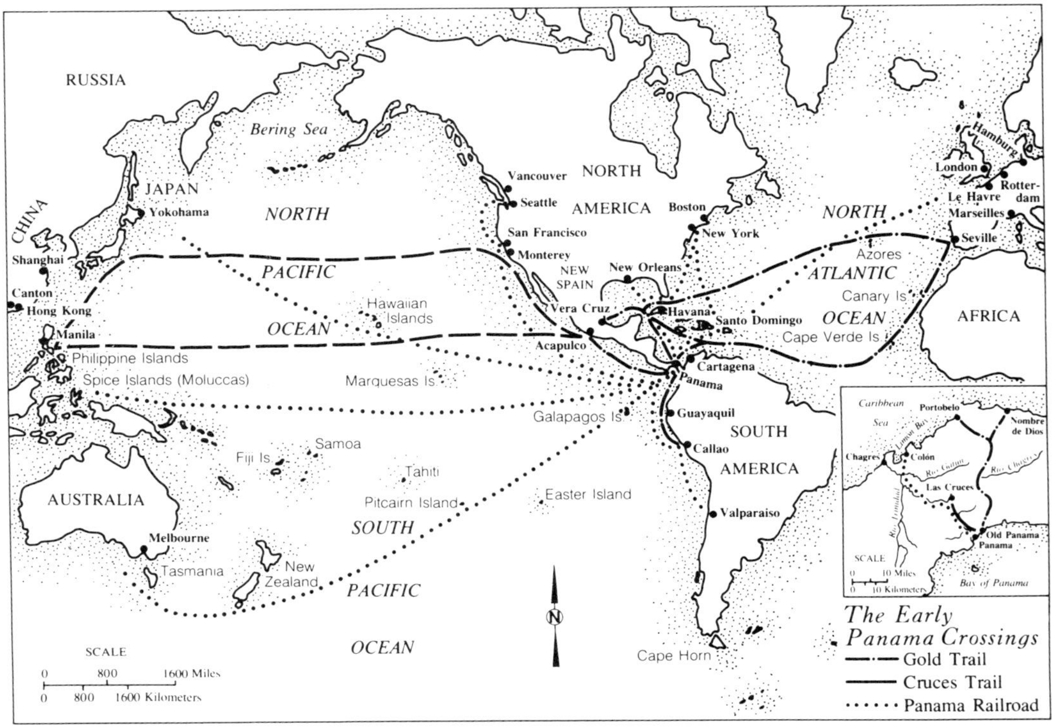

The Panama Route

—·—·— Early Panama Routes

— — — Manila Galleon Route

·········· Main Modern Panama Routes

west. What he didn't count on was running into two new continents—North and South America.

These lands had been settled for centuries by native peoples who had made their way from Asia down the spine of the Americas. These people had trade routes that ran mainly north and south, and they traveled using land trails and coastal rafts. The newly arrived Europeans wanted an east-west route, and they hoped to find a way east that was entirely by sea. As a compromise, they developed the Panama Route. This meant sailing to Panama, crossing the Americas on Panama's narrow bridge of land—called an *isthmus*—and then sailing on east.

The Voyages of Christopher Columbus

The European who laid the basis for the Panama Route was the Italian explorer Christopher Columbus. Columbus persuaded the

Spanish rulers Ferdinand and Isabella to finance a pioneering voyage out of Spain on August 3, 1492. Ferdinand and Isabella had paid for two small ships, called *caravels*, named the *Niña* and the *Pinta*. They also paid for a larger flagship, the *Santa Maria*.

Columbus's arrival in "India" is fancifully pictured here by an artist a century later. (From Theodor de Bry, *Collectiones peregrinationum in Indian orientalem et occidentalem,* Frankfurt-on-Main, 1590–1634)

Journey into the Unknown. Columbus's voyage must have seemed strange and frightening to the sailors of the time. Many people had reasoned that the earth was round, but no one had successfully tried the theory out. Columbus's last stop in known waters was the Canary Islands. His ships stopped there and his crew rested for several weeks, preparing for the unknown journey ahead.

Fortunately for Columbus, the winds and ocean currents he found carried him on a workable route. Columbus faced the same problem all sailors did in the centuries before steamships were invented. Although it is possible to steer sailing ships, they depend heavily on winds and currents. If a ship is fighting the wind or a current, a sea journey takes much longer. The ship may run out of supplies of food or water. So finding a sea route means learning how to steer toward the land you want to reach—but it also means finding the winds and the currents that will take you where you want to go.

Land Sighted. The course Columbus had originally planned would have landed him in Florida. Instead, he was confused by the calm Sargasso Sea in the mid-Atlantic. He was also misled by the sightings of birds, which made him think that land was closer than it actually was. So he turned south—and kept sailing. Thirty-three days after the fleet's last sight of land—when they were sailing in waters where no European had ever gone before—the lookout finally shouted "Tierra! Tierra!" ("Land! Land!") Columbus was triumphant. He thought he had reached islands off the coast of Asia.

Actually, Columbus had landed on an island in the Caribbean, probably one of the islands in the Bahamas. Columbus sailed from island to island, giving each one a new name. Finally, he reached a land he called *Isla Juana* (now the country of Cuba). Cuba is an island, but it is so large that Columbus thought he had reached the Asian mainland. Columbus found only small villages on the shore, so he sent some men inland to search for the great Asian cities he had heard so much about.

Although Columbus never found any great Asian cities, he still believed that the islands he had found were important. He called them *Las Ylas Indias*—the "Indian Islands." This soon became shortened to "the Indies," which was how they continued to be known to Europeans for several centuries to come.

Even though he was disappointed about not finding cities, Columbus still sent Ferdinand and Isabella a glowing report of the new land he had found:

> All [lands] are most beautiful, of a thousand shapes...and filled with trees of a thousand kinds...they seem to touch the sky...the plains and arable lands and pastures, are so lovely and rich for planting and sowing, for breeding cattle of every kind, for building towns and villages.

Gold and Slaves. Columbus noted that most of the rivers in the lands he had found contained gold. Indeed, gold was so common that

Columbus's sailors were able to exchange pieces of broken dishes or glass with the native peoples for their weight or more in gold.

Even worse for the native peoples, Columbus took some of them by force and put them to work on his ships. At first, they were taken merely as guides. Columbus forced them to go to each new village and say, "Come! Come to see the people from Heaven!" But within three years, an active slave trade would begin. Europeans would kidnap and trade for people from both the "Indies" and Africa. Eventually, these people would become slaves in European colonies in North and South America.

The Trip Home. By the time Columbus finished his first exploration of the islands, he had lost his largest ship, the *Santa Maria*. He still had two ships left—but his troubles weren't over. Columbus now had to find a route home.

Columbus was not the first to sail into mid-Atlantic waters. Other sailors had gone before, whether accidentally or on purpose. In the early centuries B.C., ancient sailors had made this trip. In Columbus's own time, the Portuguese had done it. The only problem was, none of them had ever returned.

Why couldn't Columbus just have gone back the way he had come? The reason was simple: the very currents and winds that had

This is a mid-19th century view of the Rio Chagres, which was explored by Christopher Columbus and later was the start of the Panama Canal. (Authors' archives)

brought him west would push him in the opposite direction when he tried to sail east. Therefore, instead of sailing directly east, Columbus sailed north. By doing this, he stumbled onto the Gulf Stream, a powerful current that flows northeastward out of the Gulf of Mexico toward Europe. The Gulf Stream carried Columbus and his men back across the Atlantic toward Europe. However, halfway across the Atlantic he ran into hurricanes. He was forced to stop at the mid-Atlantic islands called the Azores. Later he stopped at Lisbon, in Portugal. Finally, he got back to Spain.

Columbus never did make it to Asia. But he did discover the course that Europeans could take to reach the Americas, and the route that they could use to return. With some minor changes, sailors would use Columbus's routes for centuries to come.

The Spanish Colonies

During the 10 years after Columbus's return, the Spanish sent eight other expeditions to the new lands. Three of these trips were led by Columbus. All of them were searching for the passage to Asia. None of these expeditions were successful in finding Asia, but they did find almost all of the major islands of the Caribbean. They also explored the coast of South America, from Honduras down to the easternmost bulge of present-day Brazil. This mainland would later be known as the Spanish Main.

Columbus always believed that he had in fact reached Asia. Others, however, were not so sure. One early voyager openly stated that this was not Asia, but another land entirely. That explorer's name was Amerigo Vespucci, and his name, in the form of *America*, was given to the entire Western Hemisphere.

The Spanish and Their New Lands. The Spanish moved quickly to explore, conquer, and hold their new American lands. They realized that these *colonies*—lands that they possessed away from their own country—could be quite profitable to them. They could use products from these new lands, such as gold, and they could also send people to settle in the new lands, and then trade with them.

The Spanish made their center at a city they called Santo Domingo on the island that Columbus had named Hispaniola, from the Spanish word for Spain, *Hispania*. The Spanish sent farmers and skilled workers to live on Hispaniola. They also sent soldiers to conquer the native peoples and protect the settlers, and friars to help the settlers practice their religion, Christianity, and to convert the native peoples to that religion as well. The settlers were to supply riches to be shipped back to Spain and to explore the new lands.

Only 10 years after Columbus's discovery, the Spanish set up a colonial office and a department of commerce called *Casa de Contractaciòn* ("House of Trade"). The colonial office was to provide government for the colonies, and the department of commerce was to regulate business and trade. For hundreds of years to come this office ruled colonial activity from its base in the city of Seville, Spain.

Balboa, Explorer of the Pacific

The settlers continued to explore the new area. One in particular became known as a great explorer. He was Vasco Nùñez de Balboa. Balboa had been a stowaway on an earlier voyage, drawn by tales

This is one of the earliest known drawings of people from the New World—Native Americans from Brazil. (1505, authors' archives)

of the gold to be found in this new land. Alonso de Ovalle, who wrote a biography of Balboa, noted that the Native Americans in the area had contempt for the Europeans' love of gold. According to Ovalle, the Native Americans said:

> Is it possible you should value so much a thing that so little deserves your esteem?...Have some shame, Christians, and do not value these things.

When Europeans first arrived on the west coast of the Americas, they found only coastal craft like this balsa raft, no ocean-going ships. (From Humboldt, *Vues des Cordillères*, Paris, 1810)

Nevertheless, in 1513, the Native Americans showed Balboa how to work his way through the jungles of Panama and across the mountain range cutting through that country. He was on his way to the Pacific Ocean, a sea that no European had yet seen from the western shore of America.

When Balboa got to the highest point of the mountains, he wanted to go on alone so that he would have the glory of being the first European to see the huge sea. Balboa had his way. He went on by himself, then signaled his companions to hurry on to join him. Ovalle describes the rest of the scene:

> And when they were on the top, where there is a full prospect of the sea, 'tis not to be imagined the content they all received in admiring that vast and smooth liquid crystal.

Surprised as they were by the foreigners' love of gold, the Native Americans were even more amazed at what followed. Balboa had his men cut down trees and make huge crosses on which he carved the name of his king and queen. Then Balboa went down to the coast wearing full armor. He went

> into the sea up to the mid-leg with a naked sword in his hand, [and] said that he took possession of it, and all the coasts and bays of it, for the crowns of Castile and Leon [for Spain].

Balboa sought out the gold that was in large supply on the west coast of Panama. This gold was soon shipped back to the Atlantic coast, and the Isthmus of Panama began to be called *Castilla del Oro*, or the "Castle of Gold." Thus, finally the Europeans had discovered how to get from the Atlantic to the Pacific Ocean—from east to west and then east again, around the world. However, they still had not managed to work out how they could make the journey entirely by sea.

Crossing to the Pacific

How to Get Across? Balboa was the one who first had the idea of a canal across the Panama isthmus. But he had other ideas for crossing as well....In 1516, only three years after he first saw the Pacific, Balboa actually took apart four ships on the Atlantic side, and had them carried across the isthmus and put back together on the other side. Then he sailed them to the Perlas Islands in the Pacific, named after the *perlas*, or "pearls," found in their nearby waters.

Balboa was beheaded in 1517 because of a dispute among the colonial leaders of the area. But despite his bloody end, Balboa's ideas took hold. If Europeans could not sail across Panama, perhaps their ships could cross by land.

In 1519, Spain's King Ferdinand ordered the building of a wagon road between the city of Nombre de Dios on the Atlantic and the new settlement of Panama on the Pacific. The workers who hacked the trail through the tropical forest frequently got sick and even died from jungle fevers. They were the first of many workers who would face such problems trying to find a route across Panama.

Imports from the Incas. During the 1530s the Spanish went on to conquer the Inca Empire on the west coast of South America, the area that is part of modern-day Peru. They stripped the gold and silver from that land and brought it up to Panama. Mule trains carried it across the winding, muddy jungle path for export back to Spain. Soon the gold and silver were joined by other products from South America's west coast, including pearls, wool, dyes, tobacco, and woods, especially mahogany.

Magellan and Cortès. Although the Americas were proving to be a rich resource, the Spanish still had their eyes on the Far East. Between 1519 and 1522 Ferdinand Magellan sailed around the world. He did it by way of the Cape Horn Route, going south, around the bottom tip of South America (see Chapter 4). In the process, Magellan discovered the full size of South America and the Pacific Ocean. His journey taught the Europeans a great deal. But the distance and the dangers of that journey were too great for traders to use regularly.

Explorers kept on looking for a way through the Americas, hoping against hope for a way to sail through the great continents, rather than having to sail around them. In 1523 the Spanish king, Charles V, urged explorer Hernando Cortès to search carefully

> for the passage which would connect the eastern and western shores of the New World and shorten by two-thirds the route from Cadiz to Cathay.

Finally, it became clear that there was no such passage, so the idea of a canal—a man-made channel of water—gained support. As early as 1528 Spanish engineers proposed a canal across the Isthmus of Panama. By this time, even Cortès agreed:

> We have not found as yet a passage from Iberia [Spain] to Cathay [China], but we must cut it. At no matter what cost, we must build a canal at Panama.

Arguments About the Canal. Even though the people agreed on the need for a canal, they did not agree on where the canal should be cut. One idea, of course, was the Isthmus of Panama. But there were three other suggestions, as well.

An isthmus at Nicaragua, for example, seemed like an easier choice: it was wider than the Panama isthmus, but much of the Nicaraguan land was already taken up with lakes and rivers on which ships could sail. Another choice was an old route that Cortès had found leading across the Isthmus of Tehuantepec in Mexico. But that route was both longer and dryer than the Panama Route. A third choice was the route Balboa had taken, south of Panama, near the Gulf of Darien. But Balboa himself had called this route too hard, even though some dismantled ships were taken along this route to the west coast.

In any case, the idea of a canal soon floundered again in a series of arguments. Some people said that a canal was simply impossible. Others believed that a canal was both possible and a good idea, but could not agree on the route. Some highly religious people, including the Spanish king, Charles V, said that God would punish human beings who dared to build a canal, for that would be changing the face of the earth. Some more ambitious people, on the other hand, thought that a canal was undesirable because it would make it too easy for other countries to reach Spain's colonies.

Trade Continues. Meanwhile, traffic continued on the Panama Route from Panama eastward to Europe. South America's coasts became known and settled, and trade between Spain and its colonies continued.

Spain, however, strictly controlled this trade. It did not allow direct trade between any South American port (except for Cartagena on the north coast) and Spain. Instead, all shipping between Spain and its colonies had to pass across the Isthmus of Panama; with few exceptions, all travel had to go through the Isthmus of Panama as well. And since the Spanish claimed that all of both Americas belonged to them, trading was limited to Spanish ships only.

Battle for the New World

The Spanish would have liked to limit trade to their own ships only. However, they had powerful rivals. When other European countries realized the wealth to be found in the Americas, they moved west as well. As early as the 1520s, French sailors began to stop Spanish ships on their way home from the Americas. These sailors were known as *privateers*. They were something like pirates, for they stole gold from these Spanish ships. The French privateers also wanted to steal the valuable maps that the Spanish used to sail between the East and the West. Up to this point, the Spanish were still the most knowledgeable about the geography of the east-west routes, and the French wanted this knowledge.

While the inhabitants flee inland, French privateers raid this small Spanish settlement in the Caribbean. (From de Bry, *Grands Voyages*)

The English also wanted their share of the Central American riches, and they carried out raids in the Caribbean and on the Atlantic route. At various times during the 16th century, Spain found these routes—sometimes the whole coastline—blockaded by its European rivals.

Spanish Ship Convoys

For protection Spain increased the size of its trans-Atlantic ships so they could carry both more goods and more arms. Spanish ships sailing to the Caribbean in 1522 weighed about 80 tons. By the end of the century they weighed 600 tons or more. And by the 1550s, the Spanish had developed a large, heavily armed fighting ship called the *galleon*.

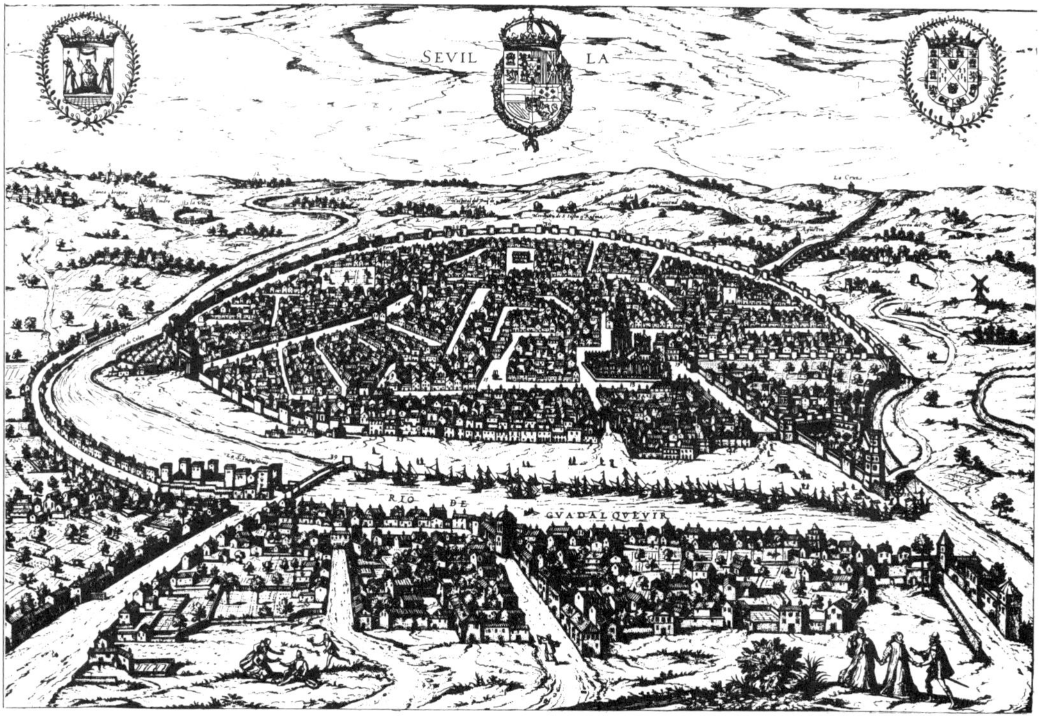

The ill-favored port of Seville, up the muddy, winding Guadalquivir River, is crowded with ships joining the *flota* (convoy) to the Indies. (From G. Braun and F. Hogenberg, *Civitates Orbis Terrarum*, Cologne, 1576)

The Flota System. Because the raiding of the Spanish ships continued, the Spanish adopted a new plan called the *flota*, or convoy system. Ships were allowed to travel only in groups, or *flotas*. From the 1560s on, the convoys left Seville in late summer and did not return until early the next summer. They still had to face pirates—but at least now, because of increased numbers, they were safer than before.

Shipbreakers. Even so, many ships never made the return trip. Some old or worn-out ships were kept in the Americas and used for local coastal shipping. Others were so badly damaged by the worms living in tropical waters that they had to be broken up when they got to port. Indeed, many buildings in the American ports were built of wood from broken-down ships.

Shipbreakers then took the iron and brass fittings from the old ships across land to other cities, such as Guayaquil on the Ecuador coast. Using these old fittings, new ships were built of mahogany for use in the Pacific waters. The metal parts were so much in demand that a captain without a profitable return cargo might sometimes sell a perfectly good, seaworthy ship to the shipbreakers.

Searching for a Pacific Route

Throughout this period, the Spanish tried different means of developing the Pacific leg of the route to Asia. This Pacific route was extremely difficult for several reasons. First, the distances were very long. Ships had to be prepared to remain at sea, with all the necessary food and water, for at least four to seven months.

The kinds of food that could be taken on a ship for such a long time were fairly limited. Sailors could eat bread and dried meat, but fresh fruits and vegetables would not keep for four to seven months. And if the voyage took longer than expected, the ship might run out of fresh water. Historian J.H. Parry gives this gruesome description: "On the longer passages hunger, thirst and scurvy could reduce a ship to a floating cemetery." (Scurvy was a disease that sailors got from a shortage of vitamin C, caused by a lack of fresh fruits and vegetables.)

The second problem with the Pacific route had to do with winds and currents, which sailing ships depend on to carry them across oceans. Lack of favorable winds and currents made the return route, from Asia back to America, especially difficult. Since the return route took four to seven months, as opposed to only two or two and one-half months to sail in the opposite direction, the presence of favorable winds was vital to make the return journey safe.

The Return Route of Legazpi. This course was not discovered until 1564 during an expedition under Miguel Lopez de Legazpi. Legazpi left Mexico (at the time another Spanish colony) and sailed west to the islands the Spanish had named the Philippines, after their king, Philip II. To return, Legazpi had the idea of sailing very far north, searching for the current that could carry him back from

Asia to America. He sailed for many weeks through changing winds and frequent storms. Finally, at the latitude of Japan, he found a westerly wind that blew him east to North America.

Legazpi's route worked, but it was long and arduous. He had sailed so far north that when he hit North America, he was in the region of California. To get back to Mexico, he had to work his way south along the coast, which meant sailing against the wind.

The Rewards of Trade. The Pacific route had proved difficult to forge, but the rich trade it opened up was worthy recompense to the Spanish. They began by basing themselves in the Philippine city of Manila, one of the best harbors in the world. In this central port, the Spanish were able to receive goods from throughout the Far East.

The Chinese, for example, were eager to trade with the Spanish, for they brought gold, silver, and pearls from America, and later chocolate from Guayaquil, in today's country of Ecuador. The Spanish also brought imported goods from Europe, including Flemish lace. The European goods were sent by ship from Europe to Vera Cruz, on Mexico's Atlantic coast. From there they were shipped overland by mule train to Acapulco on Mexico's Pacific coast. Then they were loaded onto Spanish galleons sailing for the Philippines.

The Chinese soon brought their sailing ships, called *junks*, across the China Sea to Manila. In exchange for Spanish goods, they offered silks, porcelain, and delicate metalwork. The Chinese and other traders also brought spices and Indian cotton to Manila. In addition, merchants traded in tea, drugs, and Persian rugs.

For over 200 years the Spanish carried on this trade through Manila. They would leave Acapulco early in the year and then return during the summer. For those 200 years they controlled the route across the Pacific Ocean so completely that it was sometimes called "the Spanish Sea."

Ironically, the Far East trade sometimes hurt business in Spain. Spanish traders often brought back silks from the Far East to America. When there were enough cheap silks to buy, Americans didn't want the more expensive Spanish textiles, and Spanish merchants suffered. Sometimes Spain restricted trade between Manila and the Americas to make things easier for Spanish businesses. Eventually, only two galleons a year were allowed to make the journey. These galleons were built in the Philippines of the finest teak—a beautiful tropical wood that lasts for a long time.

The Spanish were able to dominate the Pacific for over 200 years. In the Atlantic, however, their trade was much more at risk. Pirates often attacked Spanish convoys sailing between their homeland and the Americas. In wartime privateers often waylaid Spanish ships and stole all their goods. As a result, convoys sometimes stopped sailing for several years at a time.

This was a serious problem for the Spanish colonists in the Americas, because they depended upon Spain to send them both basic necessities and luxuries. Other European traders began to be attracted to the American market, eager to get some of the silver the Spanish were mining.

Ann Bonny *and* Mary Read *convicted of Piracy Nov.r 28.th 1720 at a Court of Vice Admiralty held at* S.t Jago de la Vega *in y.e Island of Jamaica.*

Among the many pirates in the Caribbean were some women, including these two: Ann Bonny and Mary Read. (From Captain Johnson, The History of Pirates, 1726, the Mariners Museum, Newport News, Virginia)

Pirates and Smugglers. Even though Spain could not supply all the needs of the Spanish colonists, the Spanish government was reluctant to allow any other nation to compete in that market—any European wanting to trade with Spanish-Americans was seen as a pirate.

In 1595 the British privateer Francis Drake certainly acted like a pirate. He landed at Nombre de Dios, ambushed the silver train on the trail between Las Cruces and Panama, and returned with his booty to England. After that the Spanish switched their port from Nombre de Dios to Puerto Bello. Nevertheless, British piracy continued. Between 1668 and 1670, the British pirate Henry Morgan attacked Puerto Bello twice. He even crossed the isthmus to take and destroy Panama itself.

Gradually, however, more Europeans became smugglers rather than pirates. *Smugglers* are people who trade illegally, either because the goods are illegal, like drugs, or because the way they are trading is illegal, for instance, if they are not paying taxes on the goods they are trading. Because the Spanish wanted to keep all American trade for themselves, anyone else had to become a smuggler. English, French, Dutch, Portuguese, and even Spanish merchants became smugglers trading with Spanish colonists in America.

Smugglers found different ways to carry on their trade. Some used illegal ports in the Caribbean. Others traded in the main ports, but pretended they were only visiting to take on fresh water and supplies. Some even came into these ports legally, acting under a contract with the Spanish to bring human slaves from Africa, but bringing illegal goods with them as well.

The Last of the Convoys. So much illegal trade was carried on that by the 17th century the situation was exactly what Spain had feared: the convoy ships from Spain could not sell their goods. The colonists' needs had already been taken care of—and more cheaply—by others.

Nevertheless, the convoys continued into the 18th century, although they did include fewer ships. The last annual convoy sailed in 1735, but it wasn't until 1778 that Spain finally opened its American ports to all traders. By that time Spain was recognizing a reality that had been true for a long time: several other European countries already had their own bases in the Caribbean. The Spanish had not been able to prevent other counties from taking their own share of America's wealth.

The Manila Trade

Spain's exclusive trade between America and Manila continued somewhat longer. Then, in the 18th century, the British decided to become active in the Pacific. In 1778, they discovered the Hawaiian

Islands, which they first named the Sandwich Islands. Eventually, the British reigned supreme in the Pacific, while the Spanish became less powerful.

The British did not win by direct military attacks; they won for economic reasons. During the 18th century powerful Spain had grown weak. First, as we have seen, it had lost many markets in the Caribbean to other Europeans. Then it lost the markets of Mexico. In the early days of the Pacific trade, the arrival of the Manila galleon in the Mexican city of Acapulco brought eager buyers from all over the country. But by 1804 three Manila galleons sat in Acapulco Harbor for more than a year. They couldn't even unload their goods, for they had no buyers. Spain had also began to lose its American colonies. In 1811 Mexico began its fight for independence. One of its earliest moves was to take back the silver that had been loaded onto a Spanish ship bound for Manila. Spain could no longer take silver out of Mexico and trade with it in the East. The last "China ship" left Acapulco for Manila in 1815, and the days of Spanish control of the Pacific were ended.

The Rise of Britain and the United States

In the 19th century there were many political changes in the Americas. The new nation of the United States, formed in 1776, was becoming more powerful. Mexico had begun its fight for independence. Other colonies in Central and South America were also fighting for their freedom.

At the same time that Spain's power was being eroded, Britain's power was increasing. The British had an excellent navy and merchant shipping fleet. Their "clipper" ships were fast and light, and soon became the most efficient on the Atlantic route. The Dutch, French, Portuguese, and Spanish were still active, though, and were soon joined by U.S. merchants. The Atlantic trade was not the only target of these European and U.S. traders. The Pacific soon attracted them as well. British and U.S. explorers began to investigate the Pacific and to set up their own routes across it. At this time, their main interest was trade with China and Japan. To reach the Far East, they used the Cape Horn Route, sailing all the way around South America, from the Atlantic into the Pacific.

At the same time, U.S. residents were pushing westward across North America, and people who lived in the Pacific coast cities of San Diego, San Francisco, and Monterey, all in California, needed supplies from Europe and the eastern United States. Before railroads were built, however, it wasn't possible to supply these western frontiers by overland routes alone, because they had to pass through mountains and deserts, making them slow and dangerous.

People living in the middle of North America (the area that is now the midwestern United States) could be supplied by ships sailing along the Mississippi and Missouri rivers. But the Far West was supplied by sea. New England traders had to sail all the way around Cape Horn to reach the California coast. This long, difficult route led once again to talk of a canal that would cut through the Central American isthmus.

Crossing the Isthmus

Considering a Canal. Certainly the 19th century was the age of canals. Many were built around the world during this century, so perhaps it was only natural that voices throughout Europe and America called for a Central American canal. Even Thomas Jefferson and Benjamin Franklin had been interested in the idea.

As before, four possible routes were discussed: Panama, Nicaragua, Tehuantepec, and Darien, along with one or two others. But opinion was divided about which was best.

In addition, there was a new area of controversy. By the 19th century, engineering had advanced to the point where there were two types of canals that could be built. One was a straight-cut, sea-level canal. This was simply like a ditch cut into land, connecting two bodies of water. A sea-level canal must be deep enough for big ships to be able to sail through, just as if they were on the ocean.

Another possibility was to use *locks*—sections of the canal that could be flooded with extra water when a ship sailed into them. The ship floated up on top of the extra water, which lifted it onto the next section of the canal. A ship floated from lock to lock, through various water levels, until it had "sailed" all the way through the canal, to the ocean. Locks were difficult to build, but they meant that the canal did not have to be cut as deeply for big ships.

Scientists and engineers argued about the Central American canal without really coming to a decision. Then events in California made a sudden and dramatic change in how people thought about crossing the isthmus.

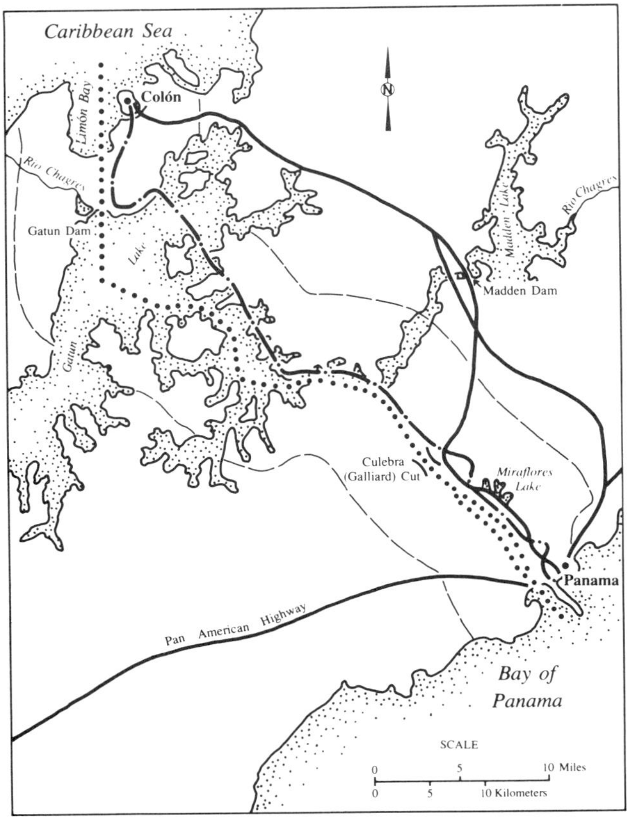

The Modern Panama Crossings

· · · · · · · · · · Panama Canal
—·—·— Railroad
———— Highways
– – – – – Canal Zone Boundaries

Gold Fever. In January 1848, gold was discovered in California. As the news spread, the rush was on. Everyone wanted to get to the gold fields as soon as possible, hoping to make their fortune overnight.

Since most of the gold rush took place in 1849, gold seekers were known as "forty-niners." The forty-niners had three ways to get out West: "the Plains across, the Horn around, or the Isthmus over."

"The Plains across" meant crossing the Great Plains, the land that is now Nebraska, Kansas, and other midwestern states of the

United States. In 1849, this was still largely uncharted territory, settled mainly by Native Americans who had come to realize that U.S. settlers' intentions were not always friendly. Many forty-niners did cross the Plains, but it was by no means an easy trip. And it took at least three months, which to those with "gold fever" seemed far too long a time.

"The Horn around" referred to the long, expensive journey around Cape Horn, the tip of South America. Many people could not afford this trip. And it also took three months.

That left just one more way—going over the Central American isthmus. This was the fastest and easiest route, and many people "voted with their feet." They sailed to all the crossing points that Central America offered on the Atlantic side. Then they crossed over the isthmus and boarded ships on the Pacific side that could sail them up to California.

Most of the forty-niners chose Panama as the easiest and fastest place to cross Central America. This cut 8,000 miles off the 13,000-mile sea trip between New York and San Francisco. Oddly, because of the geography of Central America, they were actually traveling east. Even though Panama City is on the Pacific, it is farther east than the Atlantic side of Panama. Nevertheless, the important thing was to be on the Pacific side so that the trip could be completed by sailing up to San Francisco.

A Difficult Route. The land routes across the Panama isthmus were in sorry shape. The old gold road that the Spanish had used had shrunk to a jungle path barely three feet wide. The Cruces Trail into Panama City was not much better.

Some forty-niners hired canoes to sail up the Chagres River to Las Cruces, then finished the journey to the Pacific by mule or by foot. One U.S. Army unit, which included the future general and U.S. President Ulysses S. Grant, was actually stranded in Las Cruces: the mules they had hired to carry them and their baggage were hired out from under them by gold-seeking civilians willing to pay a higher price! The medical officer with this Army unit complained:

> We had the vexation of seeing hundreds of citizens forwarded, with scarcely an hour's detention, while our men were kept at the most unhealthy place on the isthmus....[I] recommended that the whole detachment should be furnished with mules, lest the fatigue of marching over so desperate a road should

excite the disease in men predisposed to it, and they should perish [die]. This was done, but notwithstanding every precaution on our part, three fatal cases did occur on the road.

THE PANAMA RAILROAD

Since the land crossing of Panama was very hard, and since there was a great demand for passage, the railroad soon came to Panama. The railroad was a relatively recent invention, and during the mid-19th century investors were building railroads for huge profits wherever they could find cheap land and willing passengers.

Panama certainly fit the bill. Investors put together a company and bought the right to build from the country of Colombia, a former Spanish colony in South America that now controlled the Central American territory of Panama.

The Cost of the Railroad. The railroad was completed in 1855. It was the most expensive in the world, both in what it had cost to build per foot, and in the human lives that had been lost while building it. Although the railroad kept poor records, we know that thousands of laborers died—some said one for every tie on the railroad. Most of the laborers had been brought over from China and Ireland, where poverty was so great that people were willing to take even the back-breaking, poorly paid job of railroad building. The disease-filled jungle meant human lives were lost to yellow fever, malaria, and cholera.

Passengers who set sail from the east coast of the U.S. on their way west were also in danger. Many became ill and died while making the crossing or while on the ship to California. But gold fever so captivated many men that they continued taking the risk. The railroad was a money-maker even before it was finished because passengers were willing to ride even part of the way, if only they could finish their journey faster.

Shorter, Faster Journeys. Even with the railroad only half done, travelers could cross the isthmus in one day, though most made the journey in two days, spending the night at Las Cruces on the way. After the five-year job of railroad building was finished, the 47-mile trip took just four hours. And since there were not yet any stagecoaches or railroads crossing North America, the Panama route was the obvious first choice of most travelers.

Before the Panama Canal was constructed, some people thought that ships should be pulled across the neck of land by railroads, as shown in this drawing. (Compagnie Générale Transatlantique, Paris, 1884)

The Panama Canal

By the middle of the 19th century, the importance of the isthmus route was quite clear, especially to the United States. This understanding led President Ulysses S. Grant to order the first serious explorations of possible sites for a canal.

Grant ordered seven expeditions between 1870 and 1875. But Panama wasn't Grant's first choice. By now, people in the United States were well aware of how difficult and disease ridden the Panama jungle was. So the country began to favor a lock canal at Nicaragua, and the second choice was Darien—with Panama way down on the list.

The French Get Involved. A French speculator named Lucien Napoleon Bonaparte Wyse went ahead with other plans. He got the Republic of Colombia to give him the rights to build a canal at Panama. He brought in a great engineer, Ferdinand de Lesseps, the man who built the Suez Canal. While the Americans were still arguing about a canal at Nicaragua, the French moved to start a canal at Panama.

De Lesseps had built a successful canal at Suez, but he didn't understand the land and particular problems of building a canal in Panama. He also didn't understand how greatly the area's diseases would affect his workers. Thus, de Lesseps made a serious engineering mistake. He chose a sea-level canal, which meant a straight cut across the isthmus from sea to sea. This brought him great trouble.

De Lesseps thought that he had found a good solution to the engineering problems of the canal. His scouts had found a gap in the isthmus's mountain range that was only 275 feet above sea level. If this were true, a sea-level canal only had to cut through 275 feet of mountains—not the 475 feet that earlier estimates had projected.

But what de Lesseps didn't realize was that the hills around the Culebra Gap were covered with clay, tens of feet thick. When the rains came, this clay simply slid back into the holes that had just been dug. Indeed, starting to dig a canal made these muddy hills even less stable. In some places the canal workers even *lost* ground as mud slides filled and overfilled the holes they had dug.

In addition, de Lesseps saw many thousands of workers die of jungle diseases during the eight years that he worked on his canal. And he never solved the problem of dealing with the Chagres River, which at times had 40-foot floods.

Finally, in 1889, de Lesseps' canal corporation collapsed. The charges of corruption against the company caused a great scandal in France. The failure was so complete that for a while Panama was almost dropped as a possible canal route. The French kept men digging, just to keep their rights to the land, but most of the route was taken over by the jungle once again.

Manifest Destiny and Westward Expansion. The failure of the de Lesseps canal at Panama strengthened America's preference for the Nicaragua route. Meanwhile, events elsewhere in the world made a canal even more important to the United States.

At this time, people in the United States had come to believe in an idea known as "manifest destiny." Many had decided that their destiny was "manifest," or obvious: since land stretched from the Atlantic to the Pacific coast, it must be the destiny of the United States to take over this land.

In fact, once this idea caught on, many in the United States decided that it was also their destiny to expand throughout the Western Hemisphere, even into the Pacific. Thomas O. Selfridge, leader of Grant's expedition to Darien, put it bluntly: "The Pacific is naturally our domain."

Taking this lead, in the late 19th century the United States built a bridge of island bases across the Pacific. They took over the islands of Hawaii. When they triumphed over Spain in the Spanish-American War, they took some of Spain's islands in the Pacific and the Caribbean.

For the United States to control these new possessions, they had to be able to sail easily between the Atlantic and the Pacific. It was only in this way that their Navy could keep control of the territories, and their traders and merchants carry on their business. A canal had now become vital.

Back to the Panama Route. Most people in the United States still favored the Nicaragua route. But the Panama Route was also being explored. The French, however, had given up hopes of building a canal and had hired a U.S. lawyer to sell the Panama rights. And Colombia had decided to try to rewrite their basic contract with the French, taking back or limiting the canal-building rights they had earlier granted.

At that point, the French engineer Phillippe Bunau-Varilla, a survivor of the de Lesseps disaster, decided to get involved. He helped Panama to secede from Colombia, so that Panama and not Colombia would have the power to grant canal- building rights. After Panama had seceded and won its independence, one of its first moves was to grant canal-building rights to the United States.

The United States was still unsure of a site for the canal. Then a volcano erupted in Nicaragua and swung opinion back to Panama. Bunau-Varilla, who had been appointed as Panama's representative to the United States, drew up a treaty declaring that a 10-mile-wide Panama Zone would now be considered U.S. territory.

At the same time, the United States took over what was left of the French canal company and the Panama Railroad as well, using it to carry supplies during the building of the canal.

The United States Begins to Build. Engineering the building of the Panama Canal was still difficult. But the United States was now in a better position than France had been, since by the time U.S. engineers started work, in 1904, the causes of malaria and yellow fever had been discovered. Prevention and treatment plans greatly cut the risk of disease to workers constructing the canal.

U.S. builders also learned from de Lesseps' mistakes. They chose to build a lock canal—that was a good choice, both because it avoided some of de Lesseps' problems, and because of the increasing size of steamships, which were by now replacing sailing ships. A lock canal could accept larger ships.

The problems caused by the flooding of the Chagres River were solved by building two dams. This was made possible by new technology. The route chosen by the canal engineers roughly followed that of the railroad, whose track was now mostly under water. The use of locks helped control the muddy hills on both sides of the canal.

Despite these advances, many different engineers worked on the canal and then gave up. Finally, U.S. President Theodore Roosevelt assigned the job to Army engineers, headed by Colonel George W. Goethals. Even so, the project took 10 years to complete. Hardly any of the French work could be used; much of it was under the surface of the new dammed lakes.

The opening of the Panama Canal was hardly noticed. The United States had joined the world's two great oceans and opened the long-desired route from east to west at last. But the world's attention was elsewhere. On August 3, 1914, the day the first ship passed through the Panama Canal, Germany declared war on France. By the time the canal opened officially, the guns of August 1914 were booming—World War I had begun.

Modern Times

Although the world gave little immediate attention, the Panama Canal meant a major shift in world sea routes. Ships that had been forced to sail around Cape Horn now passed through the Canal in a mere eight hours. Goods that had had to be unloaded, shipped across land by railroad, and then reloaded onto another ship, could now stay on one ship for the whole journey.

The new canal was a great help to both the United States and Canada. These countries could now ship easily from coast to coast. They established a pattern of exchange between industrial goods from their eastern regions and agricultural products from the west—a pattern that continues today.

Steaming through the infamous Culebra Cut in 1915, the battleship *Ohio*'s journey from Atlantic to Pacific was at least 7,000 miles shorter than it would have been the year before. (Library of Congress)

Changes in Europe. Europe's shipping patterns also changed as a result of the canal. During the 19th century, much of the world's shipping had passed through London and Suez. Even goods from the north coast of South America were often shipped to London—

and then back to the United States. Then, during World War I, German submarines changed this pattern. Because British ships and Atlantic waters were now in danger, U.S. ships and the canal route were used more often.

Another change was the switch from sailing ships to steamships. Since steamships do not have to follow favorable winds and currents, ships on the Panama Route from Europe didn't have to use Columbus's old route through the Canaries. Instead, they followed the North Atlantic Route, using their engines to run *against* the Gulf Stream.

As ships have grown even larger in the 20th century, the Panama Canal has been widened. It now takes all but the very largest aircraft carriers and supertankers. Since World War II, growing U.S. and European trade with the Far East, especially Japan, has made the Panama Route more frequented than ever before. Greater U.S. and European reliance on imported fuel has also led to increased use of the canal.

Traces of the Old World. On the Panama isthmus itself, few traces of the old world remain. The old ports of Nombre de Dios and Puerto Bello are now poor towns rarely visited by outsiders. The old Gold Trail can hardly be seen through the tangled jungles. Las Cruces, the stopover along the old isthmus route, lies under the waters of Gatun Lake.

In their places are modern cities such as Colòn, Cristòbal, and Panama City. Beyond, in the jungle, rusting machinery covered with vines can still be seen in de Lesseps' abandoned diggings. This is a reminder of the price that was paid to bring alive the Europeans' dream of a fast westward sea route to the riches of Asia.

Suggestions for Further Reading

Bishop, Joseph Bucklin. *The Panama Gateway* (New York: Charles Scribner's Sons, 1913). Focuses on construction of the U.S. canal, by the secretary of the Isthmian Canal Commission.

Chapman, Charles Edward. *Colonial Hispanic America: A History* (New York: MacMillan, 1933).

———. *Republican Hispanic America: A History* (New York: Macmillan, 1937). Together the two make a sound history of Spanish America.

Du Val, Miles P., Jr. *Cadiz to Cathay: The Story of the Long Struggle for a Waterway Across the American Isthmus* (Stanford, California: Stanford University Press, 1940). Focuses on the political history of the canal, especially in modern times, with interesting detail.

Haring, Clarence H. *The Spanish Empire in America* (New York: Oxford University Press, 1947). A useful general history, with one chapter focusing on the commercial trade routes.

———. *Trade and Navigation Between Spain and the Indies, in the Time of the Hapsburgs* (Cambridge, Mass.: Harvard University Press, 1918). A detailed account of the Spanish Indies trade.

Howarth, David. *Panama: Four Hundred Years of Dreams and Cruelty* (New York: McGraw-Hill, 1966). A balanced account of the history of the Panama isthmus.

McCullough, David. *The Path Between the Seas: The Creation of the Panama Canal, 1870–1914* (New York: Simon & Schuster, 1977). Focuses on the actual construction, French and American.

Parry, J.H. *The Age of Reconnaissance: Discovery, Exploration and Settlement, 1450 to 1650* (New York: Praeger, 1969).

———. *Trade and Dominion: The European Overseas Empires in the Eighteenth Century* (New York: Praeger, 1971). Together the two provide excellent detail and overall context for trade and travel in the period.

———. *The Spanish Seaborne Empire* (New York: Knopf, 1966). A fascinating account; especially good on seafaring detail.

Penrose, Boies. *Travel and Discovery in the Renaissance, 1420–1620* (New York: Atheneum, 1975; reprint of the 1952 Harvard University Press edition). Very good on the early explorations.

Schott, Joseph L. *Rails Across Panama: The Story of the Building of the Panama Railroad, 1848–1855* (Indianapolis: Bobbs-Merrill, 1967). A useful, detailed account.

Schurz, William Lytle. *The Manila Galleon* (New York: Dutton, 1939). A comprehensive account of the Spanish trade with Manila.

Tavernier, Bruno. *Great Maritime Routes: An Illustrated History* (New York: Viking, 1972). Translated from the French. Contains chapters on the Spanish gold and silver routes and the Panama Route.

Wiltsee, Ernest A. *Gold Rush Steamers of the Pacific* (Lawrence, Mass.: Quarterman Publications, 1976; reprint of 1938 edition of Grabhorn Press, San Francisco). Filled with buff-pleasing detail.

2

THE INCA ROYAL ROAD

In the early 16th century, a small band of Spanish explorers arrived on the west coast of South America, the part of the continent that today is the country of Peru. This was the first time any European had been to this part of the world. For centuries, Europeans had not even been aware that the continent of South America existed. Now they were visiting a new land, a land they probably expected to be primitive and "backward" by European standards.

AN AMAZING DISCOVERY

Imagine their surprise, then, when they discovered a vast network of roads stretching for thousands of miles. Later Spanish explorers were equally impressed. More than one 16th-century Spaniard called it "the longest and greatest" road system of the world. Francisco Pizarro, the soldier who went on to conquer this part of South America, said that "Nothing equals the magnificence of this road across the sierra [mountains]."

What was this magnificent road like? We have the description of Pedro de Cieza de León:

> This was a long road, over 1,100 leagues [3,300 miles], which went over rugged mountains and along precipices [cliffs] so sheer in many places that one could not see the bottom of the chasm, some of the sides of which were so sharp that the

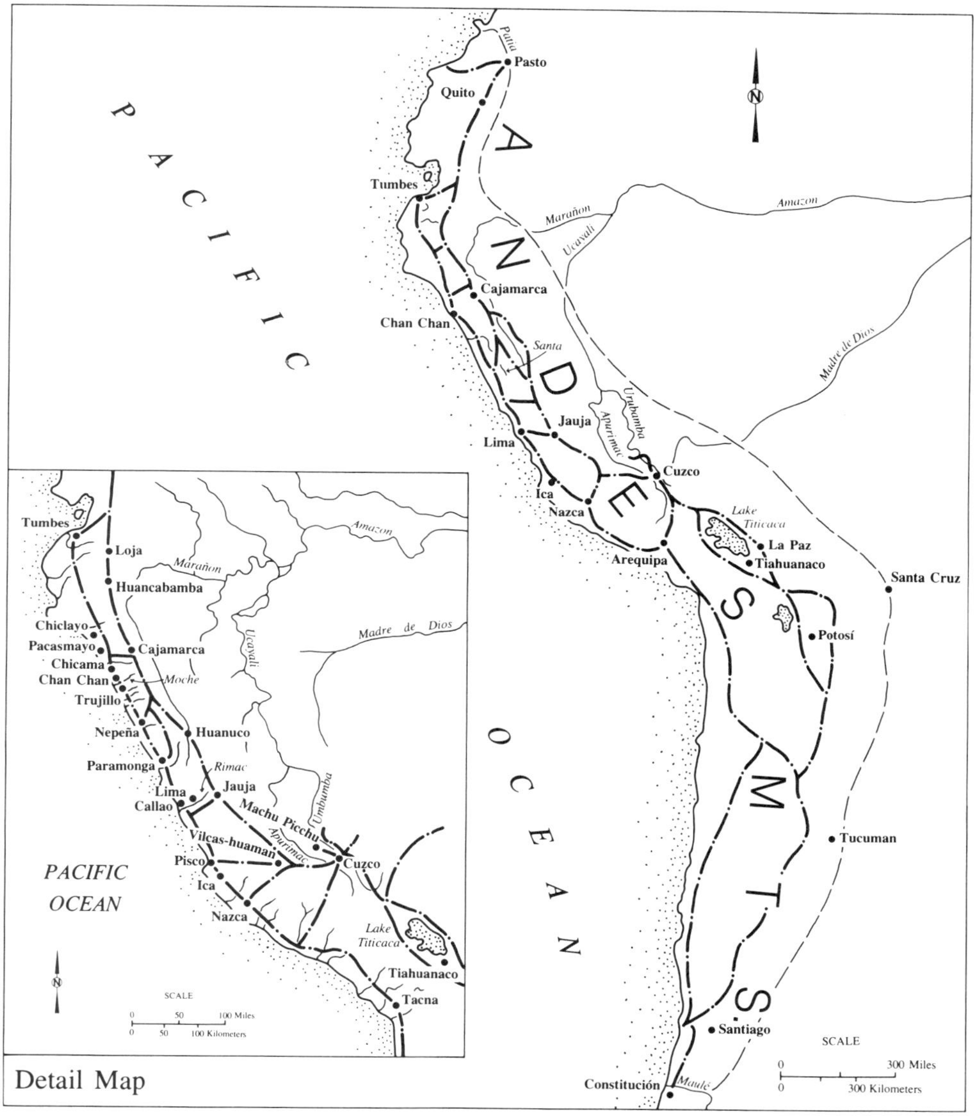

The Inca Royal Road

—·—·— Main Inca Roads —— —— Approximate Borders of the Inca Empire

road-builders had to cut through the living rock to keep the level and maintain its proper width. In other places the road's incline was so steep that they had to build steps to ascend to the top, with platforms every so often so that the travelers could rest. In other places, the road had to be forced through snow drifts and glaciers, which was the most dangerous. Yet through these drifts or through forests they built the roads level and, when necessary, well-paved with stone.

Let those who read this and have been in Peru recall the road that goes from Pachacamac on the coast to Jauja, over the craggy mountains of Huarochiri and across the snow-bound peaks of Pariacà....Let them also recall the tunnels and the twisting step-road that runs down to the bridge at the Apurimac or how the road crosses the sierrras of Paltas, Cajas, and Ayabacas and other regions of this realm where the road is some fifteen feet wide...and in the time of the Incas [the early Peruvians] clean of grass or any refuse (for they were always caring for it).

...In the memories of any other peoples I doubt that there is a record of another highway comparable to this.

The Roads of the Inca Empire

This amazing road system was part of a huge territory known as the Incan Empire. The Incas had ruled this part of South America for hundreds of years. They used this road system to maintain their control. Tax collectors journeyed along the roads, coercing tribute from people all up and down South America's west coast. Soldiers marched along the roads, putting down rebellions. Traders and merchants traveled along this road, buying and selling goods. The Incas called the road Capac Nan, or Beautiful Road.

The Inca Royal Road system covered and united a land of extremes. It crossed many different types of land, from a coastal desert where rain fell only a few times in a century, to some of the highest mountains in the world, to tropical jungle along the headwaters of the Amazon River.

The central, and longest, part of the road system ran over 3,000 miles along the ridges and across the deep gorges of the Andes Mountains. On the modern map it ran from Quito, in northern Ecuador, to central Chile.

There was another major Inca road that was part of this system. It ran along the west coast of South America for over 2,000 miles, connecting with the ridge route by a series of shorter roads, like the rungs of a ladder. These short roads followed the river valleys down

Little life is found on South America's barren Pacific coast, as here on the coast of modern Chile, except along the rivers that drain the Andes Mountains. (Hispanic and Luso-Brazilian Councils)

to the coast. A short side road also went east from the ridge route into the Amazon Basin.

The Incas took full advantage of this road system, but they were only the last of many peoples to use it. Much of the system had been constructed before the Incas rose to power. In fact, the Incas used these roads to conquer vast areas of land. When the Spanish arrived, they too would use the roads—to take power away from the Incas.

Early Times

Immigrants from Asia. When were the first roads built in South America? We don't know exactly, but we do know that immigrants had come to settle this huge continent about 10,000 to 12,000 years ago. We believe they came from Asia into North America across the Bering Strait, gradually working their way down along the chain of mountains that forms the backbone of the Americas. These mountains are called the Rockies in North America and the Andes in South America. Perhaps, too, these early immigrants were joined by others who sailed across the Pacific Ocean.

These immigrants settled in many places, some of them quite isolated. Some lived in beautiful river valleys surrounded by coastal deserts. Some moved to mountain pockets cut off from the rest of the world. Others settled in deep river gorges that could not be crossed except during the dry season.

The tribe that eventually became known as the Incas was for most of history more isolated than most. It occupied a niche high up in the Andes Mountains.

Peoples of the Coast. Perhaps because it was so hard to travel in the mountains, culturally advanced peoples appeared earliest in a 50- to 100-mile–wide strip of land on the Pacific Coast. This coastal strip is one of the driest areas on earth. As the early Spanish observer Cieza de León noted:

> Between one valley and another...lie sand wastes and arid [dry] stretches of rocks where no living or growing thing is to be seen, neither grass nor trees.

At first, the peoples on the coast kept to their river valleys. They did travel along trails between settlements, but did their best to avoid the dry, deathly desert.

Along a northerly stretch of coast, a people called the Mochica developed their culture, some three centuries B.C. This culture was centered in the Mochè and Chicama river valleys. They produced an unusual kind of pottery, so well made that much of it has survived to this day. Because there was almost no rain in this coastal desert, mud from the river valleys was the main building material. Both tools and houses were made of mud.

Below the Mochicas, south of the area that is now the city of Lima, Peru, lived the Paracas. These people are known for having created long lines in the hard, dry coastal desert. Modern archaeologists have argued endlessly about the meaning of these lines.

Both the Mochicas and the Paracas found clever ways of dealing with the dry desert climate. They developed irrigation and terracing systems: they planted their crops on terraces of earth, like series of steps, so that water ran down from one terrace to another, helping with irrigation. In these ways they made the most of the limited water supply reaching them from the Andes.

Early Trade. The desert peoples gradually developed routes along the river valleys that led into the mountains. Soon, trade began between the desert and the mountain peoples. Trade came about naturally, for each group had goods that the other wanted. The coastal peoples had seaweed, which contained both salt and iodine, important nutrients. They also had fish, seashells, cotton, tobacco, cacao (the food used to make chocolate), and possibly coca (the plant used to make the drug cocaine). The mountain peoples traded wool from the llamas they reared. In addition, the mountain peoples supplied minerals that the desert people didn't have.

Along the route in the background, couriers brought fish from the coast to people in the mountains; the *tampu* and storage bins in the foreground date from Inca times. (Victor W. Von Hagen)

These trade routes along the desert and the western slope of the Andes marked out the earliest parts of what would, over 1,000 years later, become the Inca Royal Road system. The trails were only foot trails, for these peoples did not have wheels until they were brought hundreds of years later by the Europeans. Instead of riding in carts or carriages, people walked with their goods on their backs or on the backs of llamas. Since foot trails do not have to be as smooth as trails for wheeled carts, steps of the trail were cut right into the sides of the mountains.

The Chimu Empire

For hundreds of years, the coastal cultures used this network of trails. Then, in about 1,000 A.D., the trails became invasion routes for the first empire-builders from the mountains.

The Tiahuanaco. The Tiahuanaco were a mountain people who came down to conquer the coastal land and build an empire that they would rule. Their homeland was Lake Titicaca, but they conquered the Nazca, the Mochica, and other coastal peoples. The Tiahuanacos held the coastal strip for over two centuries. Although they ruled until the 14th century, they had little lasting effect on the coastal peoples.

A New Empire. When Tiahuanaco power ended, the local peoples of the area took back control. The strongest of these was the Chimu Empire, which developed out of the old Mochica culture.

The Chimu kingdom was roughly the size of early Egypt at its height of power. It stretched for over 600 miles, from Tumbes in modern Ecuador to a region close to modern-day Lima, Peru. Its capital was at Chan Chan, a city of over 50,000 people—huge for this time in history. Chan Chan was in the Mochè Valley, near the modern city of Trujillo, Peru.

The Chimus were great builders. Following the early lead of the Mochicas, they built a large system of canals, which provided enough water to allow them to expand their farming and living spaces beyond the immediate water sources of the river valleys. The canal system made it possible for the Chimus to have much larger cities, since there was enough water for more people. The Chimus also built temples, forts, and other structures, all out of large blocks of adobe brick.

To protect their settlements, they also built a great wall. Some have called it "the Great Wall of Peru," because it was built for similar reasons as the Great Wall of China. The Chimus' great wall began in the Santa Valley and ran up into the high mountains, 90 miles from the coast.

More Roads. To connect the cities of this empire, the Chimus built more roads. They added wide main roads to the narrow foot trails connecting the mountains to the coast.

When historians look at the great network of Peru's ancient roads, they don't know exactly which roads the Chimus built: later roads, built by the Incas or in modern times, have covered up these early roads. But archaeologists imagine that Chimu roads were probably quite large. The capital of Chan Chan had regular streets and an avenue as wide as 60 feet for processions. To this day, large pyramids, official buildings, and forts remain, showing the strength of the Chimu Empire.

The main roads in this kingdom were about 20 feet wide. Sometimes they passed through shifting sand dunes called *medanos*. In that case, they were bordered by shoulder-high walls made out of adobe blocks bound together with mud as cement. These walls were built to prevent sand from blocking the road. Some sand drifts, however, were so deep that this kind of road could not be built. Then the Chimus lined the route with long poles stuck into the sand. That way, travelers would always have guideposts even if they had to walk through sand.

Llamas. People on these Chimu roads traveled mainly on foot, often carrying packs weighing 70 pounds or more, full of goods for trade. More often, though, heavy goods were carried by llamas. These hardy animals walked slowly, covering only about 10 miles a day. At most, they could carry only about 100 pounds each—much less than other beasts of burden elsewhere, such as camels and mules.

Llamas were valuable because they could work in both the extreme heat of the coast and the cold, thin air of the high mountains. They were adapted to withstand the difficult conditions of this region.

The Rise of the Incas

Peoples of the Mountains. While the Chimus ruled the coast, the mountain peoples remained isolated. They did not have huge cities or wide roads, but lived in isolated gorges, on high plateaus, and along the terraced sides of steep mountains. They spoke different languages and worshipped different gods, and had a completely separate society away from the coast-dwellers.

The mountain peoples fought among themselves for power. But until the 13th century, there was no dominant tribe or group. Then one family came to power in the Cuzco Valley, high up in the mountains between the Apurimac and Urubamba rivers. They took the name of Inca and began to defeat their highland neighbors.

At first, the Incas had some success. Then another people from the west, the Chancas, began to challenge them. In 1438 the Chancas demanded that the Incas leave their capital of Cuzco. The main Inca ruler did as the Chancas asked and left. But another Inca leader, Yupanqui, refused to leave. Instead, he attacked and defeated the Chancas, after which he became ruler of all the Incas. He was given the name *Pachacuti*, which means "he transforms the earth."

Building an Empire. It was Pachacuti who began to form the Inca empire. During his reign the Incas' reputation as great builders was born. Under his rule, the city of Cuzco was rebuilt as the capital of the Inca Empire. The buildings were made of huge blocks of stone.

Pachacuti extended the lands of the Inca Empire, which could be divided into four quarters, like the points of a compass—north, south, east, and west. So the empire itself was called Tahuantinsuyu, "the Four Quarters of the World." Pachacuti's huge empire stretched north to Cuzco, west to the Andes, south to Lake Titicaca, and east into the Amazon Basin, which was full of dense forest and tropical jungle. This area was called Antisuyu by the Incas. The name "Andes" was the Spanish version of the word *Antisuyu*.

Roads: Lifelines of the Empire. The roads into each of the four quarters were vital for Pachacuti's new government. This ruler set a firm pattern of controlling where people settled and the kind of work they did. Some peoples were moved within the empire to do certain kinds of work, using the roads that the government had built. This large, well-used network of roads allowed the government to control and monitor people's movements more easily. Where roads did not exist, Pachacuti ordered them to be built. Cieza de Leòn explained how it worked:

Now, when an Inca decided to build one of these famous highways, no great provisions [supplies] or levies [taxes] were needed. An inspector went out ahead through the lands, laying out the route and assigning Indians each to their own section, for the building of the road....In this way, with each province responsible...for the building of the road, which it undertook at its own expense and with its own Indians, the road was built and laid out in a relatively short time. When the road came to a barren or unpopulated place, the Indians that lived nearest came with the necessary tools and victuals [food], and so all was done with sustained effort.

Shown here are some of the many types of bridges devised for crossing deep mountain gorges in the Andes Mountains. (By Carlos de Bargas, from Juan and Ulloa, *Relacion historica del viaje a la America meridional*, 1747)

Wherever possible, straight roads were built. But farmland was precious to the Incas because of the general shortage of water. So new roads often went around farm fields, rather than running through them.

Bridges. New roads required the building of bridges over many rivers. Sometimes pontoon bridges were constructed. A pontoon bridge is supported by and built on floating barrels or boats. Pontoon bridges in the Inca kingdom were built on top of reed boats. Because of the floods each spring, these bridges had to be repaired or even replaced every year.

Sometimes a simple wooden or stone bridge was built over a narrow or shallow river. But how would you build a bridge over a deep mountain gorge, with cliffs plunging down for thousands of feet below?

The most important gorge to be bridged was over the Apurimac River. The Incas needed a permanent, year-round crossing that they could use even during the rainy season. Before the Inca Empire, local people had crossed the gorge in baskets pulled across the gorge on tight ropes. But they could not use this system between November and May, when the river was in flood. Heavy traffic was also not possible using such a slow system. In those cases, people had to make detours of hundreds of miles.

Under Pachacuti, one particular tribe was given the job of building and maintaining a fiber-cable bridge (that is, a bridge made out of twisted fibers, like rope). This famous Apurimac Bridge hung suspended high over the river as travelers crossed on the sturdy ropes.

Expansion. During this period, existing roads were widened and expanded. Throughout the Inca Empire, Pachacuti set up a system of *tampus*, stone buildings, a day's journey apart (about 12 to 20 miles). These tampus served as government centers for each local area. They were also good shelters for official travelers, who knew they could always find a place to rest when they were conducting government business.

In addition, Pachacuti had builders construct post houses about 1½ or 2 miles apart. Relay runners carried messages from post house to post house. These runners sprinted at top speed for a relatively short distance, knowing that they would find another runner at the next post house. In this way, Pachacuti sent and received messages from all over his kingdom relatively quickly and easily.

Within 55 years, under just two rulers—Pachacuti and Tupa Inca—the Inca Empire expanded in all directions. South, it went to the Maulè River, near modern Constitucièn, Chile. Inland, it included the Altiplano, a high plateau that is part of modern-day Bolivia. The Incas controlled the Altiplano as far as present-day Santa Cruz.

The Incas also defeated the Chimus: they forced them to surrender by cutting off their water supply. Tupa Inca's successor was called Huayna Capac. He finished the expansion that Tupa Inca had started. Under Huayna Capac, the Incas conquered the eastern slope of the Andes, and pushed as far north as the Patia River of modern Ecuador.

These are the ruins of the Inca Huayana Capac's mountain palace, Ingapirca, in what is now Ecuador. (From Humboldt, *Vues des Cordillères,* Paris, 1810)

The Incas had started their kingdom in the small valley around Cuzco. In less than a century, their empire extended over 3,000 miles. The roads they had found helped them in their conquests and in maintaining control of their territories.

Inca Roads

The Incas did not rest there, but continued building, expanding, and maintaining their road system, using forced labor, throughout their empire. The Inca engineers accomplished great things. They followed the old routes, but they widened most roads to 20 feet or more. If a narrow trail followed the side of a cliff, the Incas cut right into the rock to make a road. If an old path went up a mountain, the

Incas cut stairs into the rock, so that many people and animals could pass at once.

Roads that lay at the bottom of slopes needed drainage systems to prevent flooding when it rained. Sometimes the Incas built these systems. Other times, they simply raised the road, building it up above the ground so that water would run off it. The mountain and jungle roads that the Inca engineers forged were still dirt tracks, although they were wide and well maintained. But the roads near large towns were paved, and fitted with curbs.

The Incas also built bridges over rivers and streams. And, like the Chimu, they equipped their desert roads with high sidewalls to keep them clear of sand. Sometimes, like the Chimu, they used marker poles instead of sidewalls; travelers could at least find their way when sand had covered the roads. The Incas added another helpful marker—a distance marker. These were placed about every 4 miles. Travelers could tell how far they had come and how far they still had to go.

The Incas had an interesting custom when they journeyed through high mountain passes. Travelers who had climbed to the top of the mountain often threw a stone off to the side of the road, as if to "throw off" their tiredness. Therefore, many mountain roads were bordered by high piles of stones, called *apachetas*.

Travelers on the Roads. Travel on these roads was mostly by foot. Some of the ruling Inca family might be carried on *litters*—little platforms, like stretchers, on which some people rode while other people carried them on their shoulders. But the majority of people walked.

The Incas kept close scrutiny of who was traveling within their empire at any point in time. That was part of their way of keeping control over all the different peoples and lands that they ruled. They didn't want people going from one land to another, stirring up rebellion. So except for local excursions, only official travelers were allowed on the roads—that is, armies, officials, and other people approved by the government. Because there were so few people on these roads, armies could reach any part of the empire quite quickly. This also helped the Incas keep control of their lands.

Messengers of the Empire. Couriers, or *chasquis*, were very important to the Incas. Chasquis were on call night and day. The Incas did not read or write, but they did have a system of tying knots in strings to send messages. These special knotted strings were called *quipus*. The quipus helped couriers remember details, but most of the messages were recited from memory.

The chasquis had a special relay system. Each chasqui ran only 1 or 2 miles. Then he passed the message and the quipus on to another chasqui. That way, each chasqui could run at top speed. This arrangement meant that information could pass over the 1,250 miles between Cuzco and Quito in five to seven days—very fast for a system based solely on foot power!

The Spanish Invasion

The Inca Empire was less than a hundred years old when it had developed a system of roads, of messages, and of military control. This was the empire that the Spanish explorer Francisco Pizarro found when he and his party arrived in Tumbes in the early part of the 16th century.

The Spanish Colonialists. The Spanish had been exploring North and South America for some time—since Columbus had arrived in the Caribbean in 1492. They generally considered the native peoples they found in North and South America to be "uncivilized" and thus felt free to fight these people and to take their lands. Because the Spanish had better weapons—guns, wheeled carts, and horses—they usually won.

From their own point of view, the Spanish had many reasons to conquer these "new" lands. They wanted the Americas' gold and silver. They also hoped to find other precious goods to take back to Europe. Later, Spanish colonists went to live in North and South America. They developed huge sugar, coffee, and banana plantations in Latin America, and huge farms and ranches in North America. They profited greatly from these enterprises, and many of these profits were sent back to their home country of Spain.

From the Incas' point of view, the Spanish were unwelcome foreign invaders. Once the Spanish started to attack the Incas, they were able to use the Incas' roads against them. The very roads that had made it so easy for the Incas to control their own empire now made it easy for the Spanish to take that control for themselves. Pizarro and his party were very much impressed by the standard of these roads.

Pizarro Conquers the Incas. Using the Inca Royal Road system, in 1532 the Spanish went to the heart of the empire very quickly. Pizarro and his men moved from Tumbes down the coast road for about 200 miles. Then, in just two days, they climbed a steep road to Huancabamba, 11,000 feet above sea level.

The Incas quickly spread word of the Spanish arrival. The emperor, Atahuallpa, was returning to his own capital in Quito when he heard about the Spanish. He had just been fighting a civil war with his half-brother Huascar. In that civil war, he had been attacking the city of Cuzco, which Huascar had used as his capital.

This civil war was destined to help the Spanish cause: it is easier to conquer a divided people than one that is unified. When Atahuallpa heard about the "white men," he moved north to fight them, confident that he would be victorious. But even though he had some 40,000 men in his army, he was captured by the Spanish force of less than 200 men.

Atahuallpa agreed to pay a huge sum for his release from captivity. The whole Inca Royal Road system was put into use, transporting gold to buy Atahuallpa's release. To win his freedom, Atahuallpa promised a huge amount of gold—a whole roomful. Meanwhile, he had his rival, Huascar, put to death. That gave the Spanish an excuse for killing Atahuallpa, even after they had accepted the gold for his release. They said they were punishing Atahuallpa for killing his enemy, but really they were intent upon killing the leader of the Incas. With the nation in confusion, the Spanish set up a puppet ruler. Then, the next year, they headed for Cuzco. The Spanish path was not always easy. The Incas were not prepared to give up their land without a fight. They blocked the roads with logs and rocks. Often they burned their own fields and villages to keep the Spanish from conquering them. They attacked the Spaniards many times, in the narrow passes of the ridge road.

Still, it took only two months for the Spanish to travel the 600 or 700 miles from Cajamarca to Cuzco. They arrived in the city only one year after they had first entered Inca territory.

The Spanish and the Roads. The road system was very useful to the Spanish. When they had to cross the marshy plain before Cuzco, they were grateful for the broad and solid Inca road. Pizarro said, "After God, it was the Inca's roads that gave us victory."

Many of the Incas retreated in the face of Spanish incursion. They ran away to the wilds of the eastern Andes mountains, under the emperor they had chosen. They extended the Antisuyu Road ahead of them, along steep mountainsides, through forests and jungles. There they built new towns or added to old ones. One of these was called Machu Picchu, and it was built on a mountain peak. Their new capital was called Vilcabamba.

War. For several more decades, wars raged between the Spanish and the Incas. There were also wars among the Spanish themselves, as different people fought for their own piece of the country to rule. But finally, in 1572, the last of the Inca emperors was caught. The Spanish cut off his head, ending Inca control in any part of their old empire.

Colonial Times

From that point on, the Spanish maintained control. As we have seen, they wanted to rule these vast Latin American territories in order to take advantage of the vast array of natural resources, either by mining gold and silver, or by growing coffee, bananas, rubber, and other crops.

The Spanish Take Control. The Spanish had already begun to put their own stamp on the area. They established their own towns, although they almost always put these towns where the old roadside stations had been.

As early as 1535, Pizarro's followers founded *Ciudad de los Reyes* ("City of the Kings") on the coast, near the mouth of the Rimac Valley. For a while, this city was Cuzco's equal as a religious and government center. Eventually, it was renamed Lima and soon became the capital of the region. The city of Lima is still the capital of modern-day Peru.

The old ridge and mountainside roads were of little use to the Spanish. The Incas had been interested in maintaining control over all their peoples. But the Spanish were more interested in maintaining control of the coastline, because they wanted to continue trade between their Latin American colonies and Spain.

Also, the Spanish were not as used to land travel in this part of the world as the Incas had been. Their horses and mules could not travel the steep trails as easily as llamas had done. So the balance in the region once again tipped away from the mountains and toward the coast.

Spanish Trade. Sea trade was the highest priority for the Spanish. This interest affected the later history of the Inca roads. The Spanish maintained sea control by limiting trade to just a few ports. In turn, these ports became the most important cities.

The roads to these cities were less important than the sea-lanes. All goods from Peru had to be shipped by sea from Lima to Panama, where they were hauled overland and then shipped to Spain, using the Panama Route (see Chapter 1). It would have been possible to ship goods directly from Lima to Spain by sea, but the Spanish would not allow it. They were more interested in controlling trade than they were in being efficient.

One of the best ports in Latin America was Buenos Aires, capital of the modern country of Argentina. But because the Spanish wanted to keep control of Latin American trade, they refused to allow the colonialists to use that port. All goods from Latin America had to be shipped through Panama—with no exceptions.

This policy cost a lot of money because of the long distances that goods had to travel. Think of how much it would cost to keep a ship in good repair, hire a crew, and provide enough food and supplies for a long voyage. These costs were added on to the price of trade goods. Thus, goods in Peru cost five to ten times as much as those in Spain.

Smugglers. As a result, many smugglers began to bring their goods into Buenos Aires. Spanish, Portuguese, English, Dutch, and French smugglers used the illegal sea route from Europe to Buenos Aires, and then the illegal land route from Buenos Aires to Peru. This route was cheaper than the legal way, so these illegal goods sold for lower prices.

The territory that is now the country of Bolivia possessed some rich silver mines, and this silver was also smuggled out through Buenos Aires. Traders who used this illegal route were able to avoid paying taxes to Spain, and so this trading route thrived. The southern road was extended over the Bolivian *Altiplano* ("high mountain plain") through La Paz and the rich mining town of Potosi. From there, it went down into the valley of the *Rio de la Plata* (Spanish for "the River of Silver") to the illegal port of Buenos Aires, in modern Argentina.

For the next 300 years, this illegal route connected Latin America's west coast with the Atlantic Ocean. Spanish settlers in Peru considered this route a lifeline.

Stores like this one in Buenos Aires prospered because of the illegal trade from Peru across South America overland to Argentina. (From Vidal, *Picturesque Views*, London, 1820)

But even though this route existed, the Spanish in Peru were being exploited by the Spanish in Spain. Except for the illegal goods, they had to pay enormously high prices for the goods they bought from Europe, and except for the illegally smuggled silver, they had to pay enormously high taxes on the goods they sold to Europe. In both situations, the Spanish government in Spain made a profit. In their turn the Spanish settlers in Peru exploited the local people who were the survivors of the Inca Empire. They treated the native Peruvians cruelly, expecting them to work for low wages or as slaves.

Both types of exploitation helped weaken colonial ties with Spain, and undoubtedly led to some of the 19th-century Latin American movements for independence. Just as the 13 colonies of the United

States fought for independence from Britain, so did Spain's Latin American colonies fight for their own independence.

The Decline of the Roads. Throughout this period, much of the Inca road system went unused. The Spanish were forced to maintain the coastal roads which otherwise would have been swamped by sand dunes. But they had no interest in building new roads inland or in maintaining old ones, heavily dependent as they were on sea trade.

Most of the Inca road system eventually rotted away, and much of the eastern part of the Antisuyu Road returned to jungle, although some parts were kept up by local use. The mountain roads, too, were still partly used by local travelers. The bridge that crossed the Apurimac River was used well into the 19th century. (Later, U.S. author Thornton Wilder wrote a novel about it, *The Bridge of San Luis Rey*.)

Likewise, the pontoon bridge across the stream feeding Lake Titicaca was still used, and was replaced each year by local people. And some parts of the mountain route stayed much as they had been in Inca times, since they had been carved right out of rock. Other parts of the road were so little used that they no longer even looked like parts of a road.

The End of Colonialism

During the time that Spain ruled, the main land route was from Buenos Aires through Bolivia, to the highlands around Lake Titicaca, down to the coast, and then north along the coast. Along that route, illegal traders brought smuggled goods, much cheaper than the legal goods sold at the high Spanish prices.

Official Spanish business also went along that route, first to Panama, then to the colonial center at Lima. Up until the 19th century, the Spanish used these routes to move goods and conduct government business in Latin America.

Independence Movements. Then Spanish colonials rose up against Spain, and these routes were used by the rebels as they organized their resources against the Spanish. These bands of freedom fighters were led by people like Manuel Belgrano and Simòn Bolivar. The rebels pushed from the east coast to the west along these routes, forcing the Spanish army all the way to Lima before defeating them.

But when the Spanish had gone, warfare broke out between different South American countries. The Spanish had left many problems behind them, problems that were difficult to solve.

New Routes. During this time of war, the long-distance routes were sometimes abandoned. Buenos Aires was now free to grow as a major port, so ships were more often directed there, toward the Atlantic, rather than toward the Pacific.

Nevertheless, the old overland route between Buenos Aires and the Peruvian coast was still important. The earliest railroads in the region used parts of this route. Finally, in the 20th century, the

In marshy areas, some well-built causeways and the remains of walls dating to Inca times still stand. (Victor W. Von Hagen)

railroads themselves joined together, connecting the east and west coasts.

In more recent times, after World War II, the coastal route was chosen for the southern part of the Pan American Highway. This route picks up the old Inca road at Quito. Then the modern four-lane highway moves south along the coast, where it now covers up most of the traces of the old coastal road.

At Arequipa, one branch of the new route goes down the coast to Santiago, Chile, near the old southern border of the Inca empire, and the other branch goes up into the mountains of Bolivia and down the Rio de la Plata to Buenos Aires. These are still the main land routes in South America today.

In the latter part of the 20th century, the highland portion of the old Inca road system has in fact come alive again, not with conquerors, but with explorers. Even though the Incas left no written records, explorers have been able to find and trace these ancient highland routes using modern archaeological evidence and the accounts of old colonial Spanish settlers. The modern explorers who uncovered these ancient Inca routes have, in turn, been followed by tourists from all over the world, many of whom would agree with Francisco de Pizarro's comments:

> The royal road over the mountains is a thing worthy of being seen, because the ground is so rugged. Such beautiful roads could not, in truth, be found anywhere in Christendom.

Suggestions for Further Reading

McIntyre, Loren. *The Incredible Incas and Their Timeless Land* (Washington, D.C.: National Geographic Society, 1975). A well-illustrated combination of history and contemporary journey.

Ubbelohde-Doering, Heinrich. *On the Royal Highways of the Inca: Archaeological Treasures of Ancient Peru* (New York: Frederick A. Praeger, 1967). Primarily photographs of ruins and artifacts, with useful captions.

Von Hagen, Victor W. *The Desert Kingdoms of Peru* (Greenwich, Conn.: New York Graphic Society Publishers Ltd., 1965). Focuses on the pre-Inca Mochica and Chimu empires.

———. *Highway of the Sun* (New York: Duell, Sloan and Pearce; Boston and Toronto: Little, Brown, 1955). The story of the Inca

Highway Expedition's exploration of the road system with many photographs.
———. *The Royal Road of the Inca* (London: Gordon Cremonesi Ltd., 1976). On the road itself, and its four quarters; well-illustrated.

3

THE CALIFORNIA MISSION TRAIL

For over 300 years, Europeans knew about California—but for the most part, they chose not to travel there. California had been claimed by the Spanish, but very few Spaniards chose to settle there. The French, English, and Russians had, in their turn, also claimed huge sections of land in North America, and they often went to war over these territories. Since California was blessed with fertile lands, a warm climate, and mineral riches, it should have been attractive to the Europeans. Yet very few of them seemed to want it. Only a small network of missions—small Spanish church communities—showed that the Europeans had ever been there.

The main reasons for California's isolation were its distance from the rest of the European settlements and the natural barriers surrounding it. To the west lay the Pacific Ocean; to the east lay the Rocky Mountains and the Sierra Nevada Mountains; and between them there was a vast desert—the Great Basin. To the south lay another desert, the Mojave. Travelers wishing to come to California faced a long and difficult journey. In time, though, many became willing to make the trip.

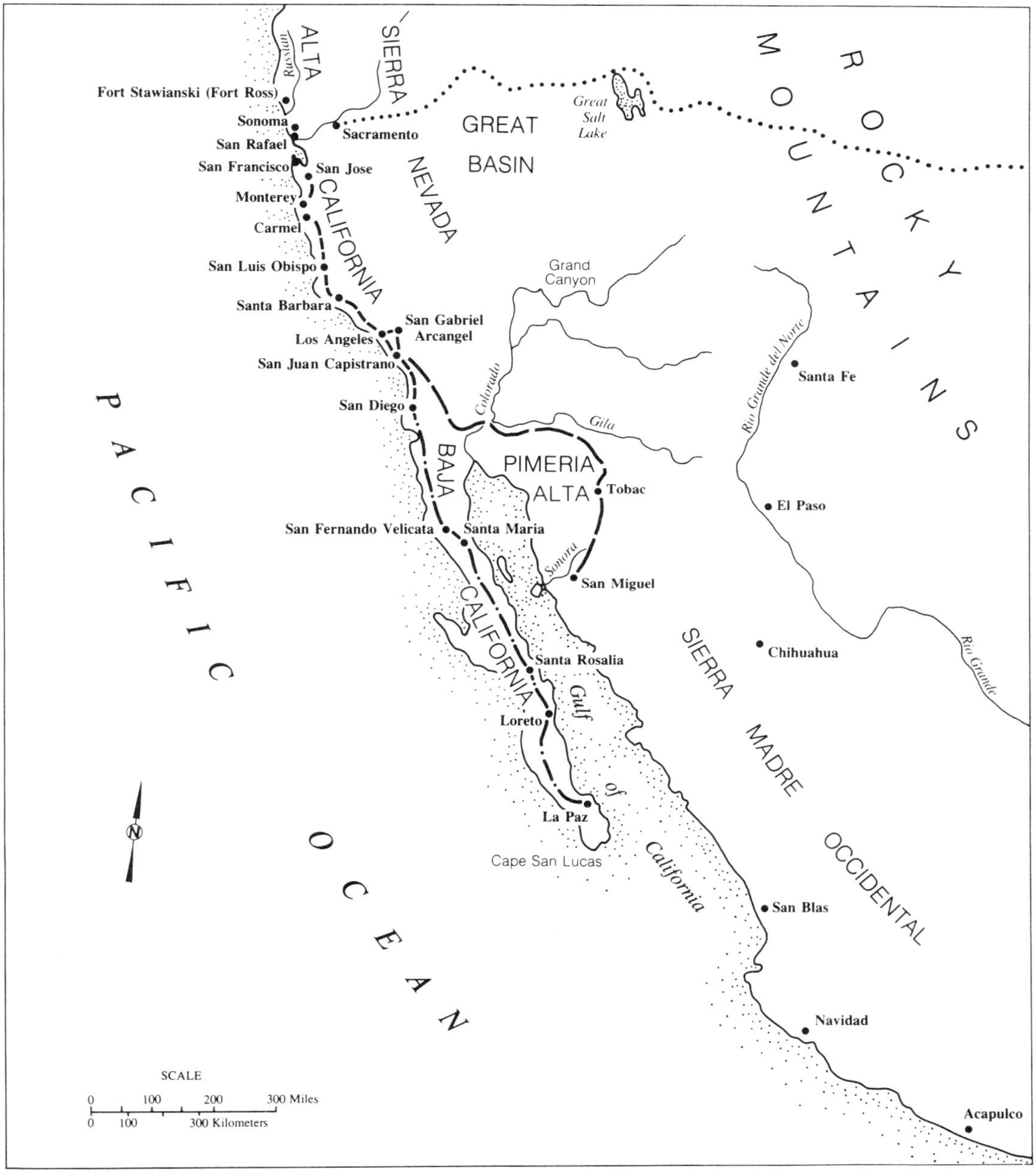

The California Mission Trail in Colonial Times

- - - - - - - - California Mission trail (El Camino Real)

—·—·— Baja Mission Trail

— — — El Camino Del Diablo (Anza Trail)

· · · · · · · California Trail

California: the Golden State

In 1848 gold was discovered at Sutter's Fort, in northern California. Suddenly, the long, difficult journey to California seemed worthwhile. Thousands of people poured into the area in the second half of the 19th century, eager to make their fortunes in gold. California was eventually nicknamed "the Golden State."

In the 20th century, millions more came to California. The early film industry put down it roots in southern California; since the sun was almost always shining there, it was a logical place to shoot outdoor movies. Ranchers and farmers came to make use of California's fertile lands and rich valleys. The visitors who once came in search of gold now came in search of land, money, or fame.

In California, Spanish and Native Americans mixed with Northern European and East Asian immigrants to form a unique culture. The tiny trail that had linked the California missions together turned into a multilane superhighway, and one of the missions on that trail turned into Los Angeles, one of the biggest cities in the world.

The story of California is a mixture of long, peaceful periods when the region was primarily occupied by Native Americans; then a difficult period as the Spanish made their first forays into the area; and finally the boom of the 19th and 20th centuries, when millions of people rushed to enter the state. The California Mission Trail is a central part of that story, and of the European occupation of the Golden State.

Native Americans and Spanish Settlers

Native Californians. The first people to inhabit California were Native Americans. They lived in various places around the area that we now call the state of California, with no regular travel or trading patterns among them.

These Native Americans seem to have spread into California across the mountains from the Great Plains—the parts of the United States and Canada that are now the states of Nebraska, Kansas, the Dakotas, and Iowa, and the provinces of Manitoba and Saskatchewan. We think that originally, native peoples came from Asia, crossing over on land bridges to North America and then spreading down through Canada and the United States. Over several thousand years, they came to live along the Pacific coast.

The lay of the land divided these early Californians from each other and also protected them from others. The mountains and deserts that surround the state kept other peoples from entering, until the Spanish arrived.

Spanish Explorers. The Spanish came to California during the golden age of European exploration. This era came of age in 1492, when Spanish rulers Ferdinand and Isabella commissioned the Italian explorer, Christopher Columbus, to make a journey west across the Atlantic. Columbus's original aim was to forge a route

Before Spanish explorers realized that Baja (Lower) California was attached to the mainland, they pictured it as an island, as shown here. (Title Insurance and Trust Company, Los Angeles)

westward from Spain to the lands of the East, which were rich in precious trading commodities.

But on his journey Columbus discovered something even better than a new route to the East. He discovered two continents that the Europeans had never come across before—North and South America.

Cortez and California. The Spanish explorer Hernando Cortez was the first to use the name "California." Cortez had claimed much of the land that we now know as Mexico. Then the peninsula to the west of Mexico was discovered. Originally, Cortez called this peninsula *Santa Cruz*—Spanish for "Holy Cross." But, according to the story, Cortez also called the land "California"—as a joke. He picked up the name from a book written by the Spanish author Garcia Ordones de Montalvo. Montalvo wrote a romantic novel in which he described a mythical island of California:

> Their island was the strongest in all the world, with its steep cliffs and rocky shores. Their arms [weapons] were all of gold, and so was the harness of the wild beasts which they tamed to ride; for in the whole island there was no metal but gold.

Cortez knew that California was a fictional place, but for some reason he used that name for the peninsula, probably thinking, incorrectly, that it was in fact an island. Today, that peninsula is part of Mexico, known as *Baja* ("lower") California. The U.S. state of California is just north of Baja California.

Early European Explorers

Juan Cabrillo. The first European to explore California properly was Juan Cabrillo. He sailed out of the Spanish colony of New Spain, the land that today we know as Mexico, in 1542, and up the west coast of North America. He got as far as the modern border of Oregon. On the way, he stopped at a place he called *San Miguel* (today we call it San Diego). He also stopped at Santa Barbara.

Although Cabrillo discovered these two ports, which are still in use today, he could not find any passage between the Atlantic and the Pacific oceans. As far as he was concerned, his mission was a failure.

Francis Drake. Three decades later, the English sailor Francis Drake came on the same search. Drake was not just an explorer—he was also a pirate. On his way north, he robbed some of the huge Spanish ships known as *galleons*. He stopped in an area just north of today's city of San Francisco, and today, the bay in which he laid anchor is called "Drake's Bay," in commemoration of his visit.

Drake attempted to claim northern California for the English, and left a brass plate behind to make the claim. He didn't adopt the name California, however. Instead, he named the land *Nova Albion*, which is Latin for "New England."

Pirates. Spanish interest in California was soon rekindled after more frequent pirate attacks on their galleons. At this time Spain was running many galleons between Mexico and the Philippines. The Mexico-Philippines trip was very important to the Spanish because it was the main thoroughfare for transporting the gold found in Mexico and Latin America. When the gold arrived in the Philippines, they bought the Far Eastern goods they wanted and shipped them back through America to Europe (see Chapter 1).

But the Mexico-Philippines trip was long and dangerous. Many sailors became ill during the long voyage. Through lack of vitamin C, available in fresh fruits and vegetables, many sailors contracted scurvy. Sometimes ships ran out of fresh water on this journey or had other problems with supplies. And now pirates had become a persistent problem.

Sebastián Vizcaíno. Because of these problems, Sebastián Vizcaíno was sent to forge a land trail along the California coast. By exploring the coastline, he hoped to find a large, safe harbor where the ships from the Philippines could rest on their trip back to Mexico.

Vizcaíno started out in Baja California, but the country was too rough and he couldn't make a good land trail over the terrain. Vizcaíno continued his search by sea. On that trip he discovered and named many of the key points along the coast. One of the places Vizcaíno visited was Monterey Bay, which he said was "all that can be desired as a harbor...surrounded by settlements of friendly Indians...with plenty of wood and water."

As it turned out, his first impressions turned out to be not at all true. But no one was to find out until several years later.

Captain Sebastián Vizcaíno was one of the earliest Europeans to explore the California coast. (Title Insurance and Trust Company, Los Angeles)

Missionaries. The Spanish eventually decided to withdraw from the search in California after having failed to find a suitable harbor. Meanwhile, other Spaniards were visiting this new land. Missionaries—people who are sent to spread the Christian faith among members of a community—were gradually moving northwest from Mexico City. They wanted to convert the Native Americans to their religion. In the process of their travels, it was the missionaries who explored California most thoroughly, and they were the ones who laid the basis for the California Mission Trail.

Father Kino. Much of the early exploration of the new trail was done by an explorer-priest named Eusebio Francisco Kino. Father Kino was the one who discovered that California was not an island. Kino was also the one who first had the dream of founding a whole trail of missions, stretching north out of Baja California.

In 1720, Father Kino founded a mission at La Paz, and one further south, at Capo San Lucas. (These locations are both in today's country of Mexico.) A mission was a small community centered around a church. It was a place where priests could live and work, and where Native Americans could come to learn about and practice Christianity.

A dusty, rugged trail connected La Paz and Capo San Lucas. It ran through difficult country, full of mountain lions, snakes, and insects. But by 1767, the trail linked up a string of missions reaching three-quarters of the way up the Baja Peninsula.

The Shift to Northern California. During the 1760s, the Spanish king threw all of the missionaries out of Mexico. All of their lands and possessions, including the missions, were taken over by the monarchy. The missionaries of that time belonged to a group called the Jesuits. The king of Spain had undertaken in 1759 to expell all Jesuits from Spain, Portugal, and all colonies and dominions of Spain.

At that same time, there was a rumor that the Russians were advancing down into California. Even though the rumor was false, it had an effect. The Spanish decided to forget about Baja California for a while and focus on *Alta* California, "Upper" California, the area that today is part of the United States.

The Spanish didn't think that this area was very valuable, but wanted it for strategic reasons—to repel the Russian advance into California. Their main concern was to protect Mexico, which was one of their most valuable possessions. They had rich silver mines in northern Mexico, which they did not want to surrender to the Russians.

So the Spanish sent Jose de Gàlvez to rule the area of Alta California. Gàlvez was charged with bringing order to the land and setting up ports at San Diego and Monterey. Gàlvez set out for California in three ships. But the winds along the coast were very strong. It was taking so long to sail up the coast that Gàlvez became convinced that a land route was necessary.

He took all the livestock and supplies from the former Jesuit missions and began to journey out from the northernmost mission in California, Santa Maria. He led a party of soldiers, and was later joined by some priests from the Franciscan order. This new group, the Franciscans, had been sent from Spain to replace the out-of-favor Jesuits. The Franciscans were led by Father Junipero Serra. Father Serra was to become a famous founder of California missions.

The California Trail

Alta California. In the spring of 1769, half of Gàlvez's party headed north toward Alta California, blazing a fresh trail along the coast. Eight soldiers went ahead to clear the way, using spades and crowbars to break through brush and forest.

After two months, the party arrived at San Diego Bay. There they found waiting for them two of their three ships, which had arrived earlier. Unfortunately, many of the sailors were dead or dying from scurvy or other diseases, and the third ship had been lost at sea. For a while it seemed as if the land of California could not be reached by either land or sea.

Six weeks later, the rear party arrived. This second group included Father Serra. They found a mission and a *presidio* ("fort") at San Diego. The group had been reunited. But on July 14, 1769, some of them moved forward again. This group's leader was a soldier named Captain Gaspar de Portolà.

A Difficult Journey. Portolà's company moved about 6 miles a day through the rough country. Every afternoon they pitched camp and sent scouts ahead to explore the next day's route. Sometimes very rough terrain or a hard march would keep the party in camp for several days.

Another obstacle facing them was stampedes. (A *stampede* is a sudden rush of a herd of frightened animals.) The mules that the party was using to carry their supplies were very high-strung. Sometimes they became so nervous that they stampeded. When they did, the party of Spaniards had to stay in camp for several days until they could round up their animals again. One week north of

San Diego, the group ran into a new problem: earthquakes. The intensity of the quakes varied, but they were always frightening. One of the officers wrote that the first one "lasted about half as long as an Ave Maria." (An *Ave Maria*, or "Hail Mary," is a Catholic prayer.)

The company gave Spanish names to the places they found everywhere they went. They called one place *El Pueblo de Nuestra Señora la Reina de Los Angeles de Porciùncula*—"the Town of Our Lady, the Queen of the Angels, on the Porciùncula River." Later the name was shortened simply to *Los Angeles*, "the angels."

Throughout the trip, their relations with the Native Americans were nonviolent and friendly. One of the officers wrote:

> The Indians came voluntarily to nearly every place where our men camped that they might present themselves to us and show us honors demonstrating the most complete confidence. ... Our men made themselves understood by signs and they in like manner indicated to us the road, the water places and other matters concerning which we required information for our guidance on the march. It was never necessary for us to use our weapons for any purpose save to obtain some game which was generally bears whose flesh had a pleasant flavor.

The Spaniards realized, too, that some of the trail they were forging was not in fact new, but that it followed older local routes.

Northern California. The party moved along a fairly easy route until they reached the site where the town of San Luis Obispo would later be founded. This is a natural dividing line between northern and southern California. At this point, they were nearing the spot where the fine bay of Monterey was supposed to be located. They wanted to find this bay, for they thought it would be useful to the Spanish ships.

Portolà's party decided to stay as near the coast as possible to find the bay. To do this they had to leave the natural trails and move into much more difficult land. A mountain range, named Sierra de Santa Lucia by the Spanish, runs right along the coast, with many cliffs dropping off to the ocean. It was not easy traveling.

For days, the Spaniards fought their way through the rough territory. Finally, they turned inland to the valley of a northward-flowing river now called the Salinas. They followed this valley, and they reached Monterey Bay—but they didn't recognize it. No wonder! It was nothing like the grand bay that Vizcaíno had described. So Portolà's party continued up the coast. From a high point on a hill, they saw something that a member of the party described as "an immense arm of the sea...which extended inland as far as they could see." This must have been San Francisco Bay.

San Francisco Bay is huge and was an important discovery for the Spaniards. But Portolà was so upset about not finding Monterey Bay that he didn't bother to explore this new harbor. He never even reported his discovery. Portolà did, however, mention finding a new type of tree with red wood, which he named the *palo colorado*. Today this tree is called a sequoia, or redwood.

Portolà had discovered a new route—the California Mission Trail. But in his eyes, he was a disgrace because he had failed to achieve his objective of finding a safe harbor. He went back to San Diego, unaware of the great discoveries he had made.

The California Missions

Father Serra. Father Junipero Serra's dream was to build a chain of missions all along the route that was eventually named the California Mission Trail. Father Serra was not the first or the only person in California to found missions, but he established most of them. While Portolà went on exploring Alta California, Father Serra and his men waited in San Diego.

The Serra party was in sad condition. Many of the men had died. And they had not converted any Native Americans to Christianity, which was the whole reason they had come. When Portolà finally returned to San Diego, he was ready to abandon Alta California completely.

But Father Serra would not give up. Finally, a supply ship arrived, and these supplies gave new heart to the Spaniards. Portolà went back via the land route through Alta California, reaching Monterey. Father Serra brought a group of men by ship to meet him there. In June 1770 the Spaniards founded a mission and a *presidio* (fort) in Monterey. The fort was supposed to provide a northern base that the Spaniards could use to defend California from Russian, English, or French invaders, but it offered little real defense. Finally, Portolà left California for good.

Father Junipero Serra laid the plans for the California Mission Trail and founded many of the early missions. (Title Insurance and Trust Company, Los Angeles)

A Chain of Missions. Father Serra, however, stayed behind. A year later, he moved from Monterey to a mission at Carmel. Father Serra wanted to separate himself from the army so that he could do his religious work by himself. He used the mission at Carmel to begin work on Father Kino's dream: a mission trail through California. Over the next 14 years, Father Serra personally traveled through California, founding a chain of missions along the route. He didn't stop his work until his death in 1784.

Each mission on the chain was about a day's journey away from the others. That was close enough for the missions to be able to help each other. It was also close enough to allow a traveler to stop at a safe place each night. At this time, the trail linking the missions was known as *El Camino Real*, "the Royal Road." In these early years, it stretched all the way from the mission at San Diego to the Mission San Carlos Borromeo at Monterey.

Even 150 years after its founding, the Mission of San Carlos Borromeo, near Monterey, was a modest settlement, with post riders arriving on the Mission Trail. (By Capt. W. Smyth, R.N., from Alexander, Forbes, *California: A History*, 1839)

Many of the missions Father Serra built still survive today. They were the basis for many Californian towns. Father Serra's missions included San Antonio de Padua, about 70 miles south of Monterey; San Gabriel Arcangel, near Los Angeles; San Luis Obispo; San Juan Capistrano; and Santa Clara.

Father Serra and his men also pushed the California Mission Trail to the north, where they built Mission San Francisco de Asis. This was the mission named after Saint Francis of Assisi—and the beginning of the city of San Francisco.

San Francisco and the Golden Gate. The mission was located on the southern point of the "Golden Gate"—the high cliffs that face each other across the great bay. The site was such a good one that soldiers also built a presidio there to guard the mission. Finally, people began to realize what a potentially good harbor the bay was. In 1776, Father Pedro Font wrote this description:

> The port of San Francisco...is a marvel of nature, and might well be called the harbor of harbors, because of its great capacity and of several small bays which it enfolds in its margin....Indeed, although in my travels I saw very good sites and beautiful country, I saw none which pleased me as much as this.

In later years, other priests crossed the bay. On its northern shore they founded the Missions San Rafael Arcangel and San Francisco Solano de Sonoma. These missions were farthest north on the thousand-mile trail. The trail reached as far south as the southern tip of Baja California.

Hardships of the Trail. This key route was much more like a trail than a road. It had no bridges. In the rainy season, there was no place for water to drain away, for the trail was not raised on a causeway or a graded (sloping) crossing. In the south, the trail ran along the coast, near Santa Barbara. During high tide, this section was almost completely under water.

The trail was tramped down by the feet of priests, Native American converts to Christianity, and livestock driven back and forth to supply the new missions. Besides being difficult, it was dangerous. The majority of Native Americans living in California did not welcome the foreigners who took control of their land and tried to convert them to another religion. Here is how the *comandante* ("commanant") at Monterey, Pedros Fages, described the difficulty:

> In order to travel and transport goods from San Diego to Monterey it is necessary to pass twenty or more Indian towns either directly through them, along their borders, or at least within sight of them at about gunshot distance and there are numerous cliffs, bluffs, and difficult passages where the natives might, to advantage, dispute the way and even prevent travelers from passing. Instances of this are not lacking. For example, in the year '72 they threw stones and darts at me when I was going down to San Diego at a place which we call

El Rincon; the Indians took advantage of an opportunity to surprise me and my escort when we were occupied in effecting a difficult passage, and we found ourselves in such straits that it was necessary, assuming the defensive, to punish the boldness of the insolent [proud and defiant] fellows, killing one or more of them but losing none of our men. Since then they have shown some caution but whenever they see a small number of travelers not well armed the Indians do not hesitate to try their fortune. It is plain to see that there is no means of forfending [avoiding] these injuries [except]...to establish presidios and missions in suitable places.

The first Spaniards in California had received a different, more friendly welcome from the Native Americans. But by this time, the native peoples had begun to distrust and fear the newcomers. They were no longer willing to allow the Spaniards to do whatever they pleased.

Colonial Times

An Age of Revolutions. In 1776, the 13 colonies in the eastern part of North America revolted against the British, and achieved independence as a new country—the United States.

This revolution marked the beginning of a series of revolts all over the world. In 1789 the French rose up against their king and queen, changing their monarchy (where a king or queen rules) to a republic (where rulers are elected). Likewise, many other colonies, including those belonging to Spain, began to think about winning freedom for themselves. Yet even in the midst of these uprisings, California was left alone, and it remained undisturbed by political turmoil.

Life in Early California. The Spanish priests in California continued to convert Native Americans to Christianity. These converts were generally not treated very well; some were kept almost like slaves, for the priests locked them up each night, hoping to keep control over them. The Native Americans were treated even more harshly by Spanish soldiers. The soldiers understood that they were fighting a war and that the winner would eventually control the land of California. During the fighting, Native Americans often turned to the church for some protection from the military violence.

Visitors were rare in California, because the region was so inaccessible. Sometimes a ship would land in a Californian port, but sometimes years would go by without even one stopping.

In the late 18th century, visitors on the Mission Trail were so rare that they received a full-scale welcome, as did the Comte de La Pérouse in 1786. (Museo Naval, Madrid)

The colonists in California did not have an easy existence. When there were visitors, the Californians tried to trade their own possessions for the goods they needed. They had to trade goods, for they had no currency that the visitors wanted. The money they had was good only in California.

Even though today California is part of the United States, it was quite a separate place in 1776. Imagine the great distances between the two areas—vast distances inhabited by Native Americans, with no established paths of communication across the continent. It was only in 1796, in fact, that the Californians learned that the rumors were true: there really was a new nation, the United States of America, and it had declared its independence 20 years earlier.

Spanish Control. Gradually, as travel became easier, California began to receive more and more visitors. However, the Spanish continued to exert control over all incoming visitors, and those who sailed into a California port were not allowed to travel inland.

The Spanish continued to fear a Russian attack. The Russians had been exploring further north; however, they were more interested in trapping animals for fur than in permanently establishing colonies in the United States or California. They had been edging farther south, and had set up a southern base, at Fort Stawianski, just north of the Russian River. The Spanish called this base *El Fuerto de Los Russos*, "the Fort of the Russians." Later the name was changed to Fort Ross.

The Russians needed food supplies for their trappers, who had many furs but no crops. They set up trade with the Spanish, who were happy to have the business but still wary of Russian intervention. Nevertheless, they did not take any active steps to push the Russians out of Fort Stawianski.

A Time of Confusion. Technically, California was part of the colony of New Spain, which we now know as Mexico. In 1821 New Spain finally won its independence from Spain. This new arrangement brought a time of confusion for California. Even though it was part of Mexico, that new country did not have the resources to administer California, especially not the faraway land of Alta California.

Pirates became frequent visitors to the Californian coast, and more than once, women and children were sent away from the coastal areas along the Mission Trail to the safer inland missions. Generally, the pirates didn't bother to go inland, for that land was still seen as wild.

Up until this time, the Mission Trail had connected Baja California with Alta California. But with the onset of confusion after Spanish departure and the threat of piracy, the trail fell into disuse. Upper California became remote and relatively unvisited. As late as 1800, it was still primarily Native American country. In that year there were only 740 Spanish males of all ages in Baja and Alta California combined.

A Rough Trail. In some places, the Mission Trail had been made wider by all the people who had passed along it. But generally, conditions along the trail were very poor. In some places the road ran almost into the sea. In other places, it ran quite near the edge of sheer cliffs that dropped quickly to the ocean. The means of travel were also rough. Mostly, people walked on foot or rode horses and mules. Sometimes they drove wooden-wheeled *carretas*, or "ox carts." Even at this time the ox cart was considered quite old-fashioned.

Among the dangers—and food sources—along the California Mission Trail in its rougher days were wild animals, like this bear being lassoed by some Californians. (*History of the United States*, 19th century)

TRADE

The "Americans." By this time people from the newly formed United States had taken the name "Americans" for themselves. It was these Americans who gradually became California's main trading partners. Boston ships of the 1820s sailed from the Atlantic around Cape Horn at the tip of South America to reach the Pacific. Their final goal was the rich China trade at the other end of the Pacific, but they often stopped in California along the way. The Californians had been cut off from both Spain and Mexico and were quite eager to trade with these new Americans.

The Californians, for their part, had a huge surplus of cattle. They traded hides and tallow, a kind of fat used for making candles. Since the United States valued these products, the trade quickly developed.

Whenever a Boston ship sailed into Monterey, leaflets announcing its arrival were distributed up and down the Mission Trail. Agents from the ship would follow the leaflets, trading up and town the trail at missions and ranches. Even the priests joined in the trade. They set up small stores selling various items. The ranchers, of course, depended on this market for their cattle products. The Mission Trail had become a trade route.

Sometimes, though, the Boston traders took advantage of these Californians, who were not yet used to trading. Sometimes the Bostonians made a profit of as much as 300% on their goods.

The Riches of California. Gradually, the Americans began to realize the treasures that could be found in California—rich land for ranches and farms, a beautiful climate, and a peaceful life. Many Boston traders and sailors left their ships and settled in California. Some married into the now-wealthy Spanish families there.

In 1833 the United States set about securing more Californian resources for themselves. At this time the Franciscan monks had extensive holdings of land and goods, for there were many Franciscan missions in California. A law was passed giving half of the Franciscans' wealth to the United States. The other half theoretically went to the Native Americans, but they were soon cheated of most of it by various traders. The missions had lost most of their power.

Changing Times. The change of power made a huge difference along the Mission Trail. Before, all travelers, even strangers, were always sure of a welcome, a good meal, and a clean, safe bed in either a mission or a ranch. Afterward, the mission buildings were still there, but they and their grounds were no longer kept in good repair. Travelers had to settle for flea-ridden beds and poor food—and they had to pay high prices for these poor accommodations.

Meanwhile, refugee Indians, whose land had been taken from them, became robbers along the Mission Trail. They were soon joined by local California outlaws. Some of these "outlaws" were actually rebels, part of a failed revolt for freedom from Mexico fought in 1831 at Cahuenga Pass. For all these reasons, the Mission Trail had become dangerous to those traveling on it.

In 1840, the Russians finally left Fort Ross, ending their period of incursion into North America. Americans, however, kept coming into California, either by ship or by land. Mexico still controlled this territory—but it would not do so for long.

America Expands

Gradually, throughout the early half of the 19th century, Americans moved into the Southwest, fighting both the Mexicans and the Native Americans who lived there. Eventually, they took over Texas and much of the Southwest.

Finally, in 1846, some Americans, led by Captain John Frèmont, claimed California for the United States. For the next two years various small battles were fought on or near the California Mission Trail. The question was settled in 1848, under the treaty of Guadalupe Hidalgo. This treaty gave the United States all the territory north of a line 10 miles south of San Diego. This was roughly the land that had been known as Alta California.

From then on, Alta California was known simply as "California." Baja California remained part of Mexico, keeping its old name, as it does to this day.

Gold Rush Days

The Americans had been far more fortunate than they could ever have imagined in gaining California, for in 1848 gold was discovered there. The great movement of people "rushing" out West to get their share of the precious metal soon became known as the "Gold Rush."

One result of the Gold Rush was that California was quickly incorporated as a state in the Union in 1850. Another result was that thousands of people settled in this western state, which until then had been isolated and sparsely populated.

The Gold Rush Boom. At first, many of the towns along the Mission Trail were emptied as the people who had lived there rushed to the gold fields. But some soon realized that they could become just as rich selling goods and services to the people who were looking for gold.

Small towns along the coast suddenly became "boom towns"—towns that grew so fast it seemed as though they had doubled their size overnight. Hotels, restaurants, gambling houses, brothels, and stores were quickly built to provide services and goods for the miners, or "prospectors" who had come West.

Bandits and Justice. During this boom, the Mexicans and Native Americans living in California were treated more poorly than ever before. Although land had been granted to these people, many were driven off because they could not "prove" that they were owners. Those who drove them off wanted to make a huge profit from the land, either by mining gold on it or by selling it to other prospectors.

Most of these Mexicans and Native Americans were driven into poverty. Some became bandits to survive. They joined the already large groups of thieves living in the hills along the California Mission Trail, robbing the travelers who passed. In retaliation, townspeople along the trails sometimes formed *vigilante* groups who guarded the towns.

A Rough Road. The California Mission Trail itself was in terrible condition during this period. Outside of the towns, the route was simply a line of wheel ruts cutting through fields or sand dunes. On both sides of the trail were wide paths where drovers (people driving cattle) herded their animals. If travelers wanted to cross a river, they could take a ferry. But ferries charged huge prices in these boom times. To get across the Golden Gate, for example, cost $50—an enormous amount of money in those days.

In addition, earthquake damage was hardly ever repaired. Roads in the populated or heavily traveled areas were kept up to some extent. The suburbs of San Francisco, for example, were served by a 40-foot wide toll road of planks with a hard- packed surface. But in most places the California Mission Trail was still merely a trail.

Stagecoach Days

Delivering the Mail. In 1858 regular stagecoach service came to California. Before that time, mail from the eastern United States had been sent by sea to Central America, where it crossed the isthmus of Panama by land and then was sent by sea again up the Californian coast. Mail from the Southwest and from Mexico was sent overland by mule train.

The new stagecoach service from the East made a big difference to both mail services. The new stage line followed the "Ox-Bow Route" from St. Louis along the southern border of the United States to San Diego. Then it went up the California Mission Trail. This

Carrying passengers and the vital mail, the stagecoach pounds the ground to keep its schedule along the California Mission Trail. (*Stage Arriving in California*, by Einar Petersen, Title Insurance and Trust Co., Los Angeles)

route was also called the Butterfield Southern Overland Mail Route, named after the stagecoach line itself.

The traffic and the new business brought by the stagecoaches were very attractive for some southern California towns. Los Angeles and Santa Barbara in particular profited from the many people who were coming to California now that travel was easier.

Some towns wanted to make travel even easier for these newcomers. They passed bond issues to pay for improving their roads. (A bond issue is when a town sells shares or *bonds* to private citizens. The town uses the money from the bonds to improve a road or conduct some other public business. The town pays interest on the bond, or buys it back at a higher rate, so that the citizen makes a profit.)

Advertising. With stagecoaches, the age of advertising came to California. California was at the far edge of the Wild West, which many people of the time found romantic. Writers made the most of this romance when they described the Golden State.

Often, the ads had little to do with reality. Here is one from a stagecoach company, urging people to take a ride to the West:

> There is no more charming drive in California than that from San Francisco to San Jose and as one is whirled rapidly through

> the oak openings and across the level plains...he finds that pleasure is united with business and wonders why he has never made the trip before.

Of course, this ad exaggerates the wonders of California somewhat. "Pleasure" is hardly the word to describe a stagecoach ride, which was dusty, bumpy, and either too hot or too cold. The coaches were usually the Concord type, in which the coach was slung on two leather straps hanging above the wheels. Mark Twain called it "an imposing cradle on wheels." This meant that the coach swayed back and forth. The idea was that even if the wheels hit bumps or holes in the road, the coach would not bump along with them. But the swaying of the coach made many people seasick.

However, travelers in California had little choice. The California Mission Trail was just about the only road in California, other than a few local ones.

During this period, Sacramento was the focus of the stage lines. It was close to the gold fields, and it connected with both the northern overland route from the East and the route to Oregon and Washington. But with the end of the Gold Rush and the coming of the railroad, San Francisco would become the focus once again.

The Railroads

The Iron Horse. The coming of the railroads was to change patterns of travel all over the world. Suddenly, the "iron horse" made it possible for people to travel in relative comfort, avoiding the long difficult journeys on foot, horseback, or stagecoach. Faraway places became a matter of only a few weeks' journey. Goods that had been too bulky to carry by land could suddenly be sent by rail.

These changes also affected the United States, for suddenly the journey between the East and the West was much faster and easier. Towns sprang up all over the country to take advantage of the visitors and trade carried by rail. The railroad brought a new kind of boom across the United States.

Whenever it was found out that a railroad was coming to a certain area, that area's land became very valuable. Either people wanted to own land that they could sell again to the railroad, or they wanted to own land near the railroad station to take advantage of the business it would bring.

Rumors of the coming railroad caused a huge land boom along the California Mission Trail, since, at the time, it seemed the logical route for a railroad. But then the boom collapsed, for the railroad company changed its plans. Instead of laying the railroad along the coast, where the Mission Trail ran, the Southern Pacific Railroad decided to run its trains from Los Angeles across the Mojave Desert, and up the central San Joaquin Valley.

The New Paradise. Nevertheless, coastal California continued to hold the most attraction for the residents of the East. Southern Pacific hired a huge staff of writers, lecturers, and publicists (people who write and spread publicity) to make California look like a paradise. That way, the railroad hoped, California would attract many new tourists. The tourists would want to ride on the railroad—and the railroad company hoped to make a huge profit from the increased number of travelers.

The advertising campaign succeeded. Tens of thousands of people believed that California was paradise on earth. They came to the state to take up farming. Cities exploded off paper into reality as new businesses were founded to serve all these new residents. Cities like Los Angeles and San Diego grew with amazing speed: up to one or two thousand new people per month.

It wasn't just farmers who came to California. The rich and the famous decided that sunny California was the place to come for vacation or for rest. Along the coast, great resort hotels were built for the wealthy. A few years earlier only raw frontier had existed. Now hotels like the Del Coronado in San Diego, the Arlington in Santa Barbara, the Palace in San Francisco, and the Del Monte in Monterey drew presidents and princes.

All in all, about 1 million people came to California, drawn by the railroad campaign. Not all of them stayed. But most of those who did settled near the old California Mission Trail.

Bicycles and Cars

Transportation was changing quickly. After the railroads came, stagecoaches were reduced to short hauls. They might take tourists from their hotels to famous sightseeing spots, but that was all. Then new means of transportation were invented, leading to much improved roads.

But for the two bicyclists and the telegraph poles, this road—Cahuenga Pass through Hollywood—in 1899 is much as it was in the early days of the California Mission Trail. (Security Pacific National Bank Photography Collection, Los Angeles Public Library)

Bicycles. First came the bicyclists. By the 1880s, the bicycle had become a popular means of transportation. Bicyclists formed an organization to push for better highways so that riding would be easier. Bicyclists also produced probably the first real road map of the California Mission Trail. This was published in their magazine, *The American Bicycler*.

Automobiles. By 1900 the cyclists were joined by drivers of the first widely available cars. Car owners also formed their own club to lobby for highway improvement. Soon, gasoline was sold along the Mission Trail. In those early days of driving, there were no service stations. The old livery stables, which had supplied horses and their riders, now turned to selling gas. Some people also bought gas in general stores.

Automobilists became excited at the new possibilities opened up by cars. They began to set speed records. One early speed record seems like a long time today, but it was short then: only 13 hours from Los Angeles to Santa Barbara!

Where buggies and bicycles once ruled, cars and paved roads began to dominate, as here at Cahuenga Pass in 1928. (Title Insurance and Trust Co., Los Angeles)

Earthquake. Then, in 1906, the San Francisco Earthquake hit northern California. Much of San Francisco was destroyed in the quake. In addition, the northern part of the California Mission Trail was hit. The quake split the highway open to gaps of up to 20 feet. In many places, the road was unpassable because of rocks and mud slides.

This frightening event drove many people down to Los Angeles. They told stories about the quake—and about the terrible condition of the California Mission Trail. Their stories encouraged public support for highway improvement. People in towns along the route donated their own labor to build the road, fill in holes and ruts, and mark heavily damaged areas. The road was still only a dirt road, though.

By the time of World War I, more horses were to be found on the lots of southern California's movie studios than on the California Mission Trail. Livery stables were replaced by service stations that sold gasoline and fixed automobiles. In place of the old stagecoach bandits, people now feared car thieves who stole vehicles and took them across the border to resell in Mexico.

Road Improvements. In the early 1920s, cars were even more abundant, and this led to more large-scale road improvements. With federal government funding, the Mission Trail began to be paved.

Over the decades the Mission Trail had changed from a zigzag path connecting missions to a straighter road connecting the towns and cities that had grown up along its route. Engineers now made the Mission Trail a modern road. They made it wider and smoother. Sometimes they cut into rock along the cliffs. Road bridges were built out of concrete. Occasional disasters slowed their progress. There was a large earthquake in Santa Barbara in 1925, and a dam-burst in the Santa Clara Valley in 1928. However, the momentum to improve the road kept on.

In modern times, the road was given a number instead of a name. The branch of the Mission Trail from San Diego to Los Angeles and then north into the San Joaquin Valley—the route the railroad had chosen—was labeled U.S. Route 5. The old El Camino Real from Los Angeles north along the coast became U.S. Route 101.

Signs of the Times

Other signs of modern times began to appear. In 1925 the first motel in California was built at Route 101 at San Luis Obispo. Before, people had stayed in hotels located in towns or communities and geared toward stagecoach or railroad travelers. Now, "motor hotels" were built along the highway to accommodate drivers. Buses came into use along the route as well. Soon they were carrying more passengers than the Southern Pacific Railroad. Heavy trucks began to run on U.S. Route 101, hauling produce from Californian farms.

In the 1930s the United States went through the Great Depression. This was a time when there was high unemployment and great poverty throughout the nation. Hundreds of thousands of people left the states of the Midwest, where poverty was at its worst because of severe droughts that had blighted the land and therefore the living of most of the farmers. These refugees flocked to California, believing that it was a land of plenty where they could find work. Many of them had to leave their cars by the side of the road when they ran out of money to buy gas or make repairs.

Now hitchhikers and hobos wandered along Route 101. Many had been stranded, paid to drive new cars out West with the false promise of being given return fare to go back home. Under President Franklin Roosevelt, the federal government set up camps along Route 101 to give the homeless people a place to stay and something to eat. Other federal government projects tried to increase employment by hiring people to work in public services. Many people were employed to repair the highway, which now needed more repairs than ever before because of the increased traffic.

One more change was made during this time. In 1937 the Golden Gate Bridge across San Francisco Bay was completed. Before the bridge was built, people had used ferries. Now they could drive from the California Mission Trail right on to the rest of U.S. Route 101, which extended north to San Rafael, Sonoma, Oregon, and Washington.

Modern Times

World War II. The next war brought even greater changes to the old Mission Trail. Because World War II was fought against Japan in the Pacific, California became the focus of the Pacific war effort. Major naval bases were developed at San Diego, Los Angeles, and San Francisco. Training centers and defense plants sprang up in those areas, too. Millions of new people came to work in the plants, to serve in the armed forces, and to visit those heading for battle.

Not for the last time, California became extremely crowded—and traffic became congested, as well. There were plans to rebuild Route 101, but a project so big could not be undertaken while the country was at war. However, Route 101 continued to serve as a major pathway of transport and communication throughout the war. The beaches along the highway were closed with barbed wire, because of fears of an enemy attack.

Many Japanese immigrants had settled and raised families along the Mission Trail. Because the United States was now at war with Japan, this served as an excuse to drive these Japanese-Americans off their land, even though many of them were U.S. citizens and had even been born in the United States. Some of their sons even fought in the U.S. army against Japan while the families were sent to detention centers because of their "threat" to U.S. security.

After the War. By the end of the war, California's population had grown to almost 9 million people. Throughout California's history, northern California had always been more important because it was richer in natural resources. Now a combination of the movie industry and military activity had shifted the population center to southern California.

In 1945 the California Mission Trail was still heavily used—and still badly in need of improvement. The road was little more than a city street. It had cross streets, traffic lights, left and right turns, and sometimes toll stations to collect *tolls*, or taxes, for using the highway. All of these things made travel on the route very slow.

The First Freeway. Engineers came up with another new idea: the first modern highway, or freeway. They decided to build a multiple-lane road with no stops, turns, or crossings, all the way from San Diego to San Francisco. You could get on and off the road by ramp so that traffic would not be slowed down. Shrubbery would be planted in between the three lanes going north and the three lanes going south to prevent accidents and to cut down the glare from oncoming headlights.

When the freeway was approved, there was another land boom along Route 101. People expected to be able to sell their land again at huge profits. Many, however, were disappointed because they found out that the road was going to take a straighter route to bypass some old towns. Many small business owners had made their living from selling goods to drivers along Route 101, but these now went out of business as the new freeway was constructed.

Building the road took 15 years, from 1945 to 1960. The cost was so high that freeways were sometimes called "gold-plated highways." But critics also complained that these expensive roads should have been built even wider! By 1954 the Hollywood Freeway was used by 168,000 vehicles a day—and the number kept going up.

For better or for worse, California's multilane, limited-access freeway system seems here to stay. (California Department of Transportation)

Now the California Mission Trail has changed from a dirt path through cliffs and canyons into a smooth, paved freeway. Much of the route, however, continues to follow the early trail forged by Father Serra and the early explorers who were the first people to connect southern and northern California.

Suggestions for Further Reading

Bolton, Herbert E. *The Spanish Borderlands: A Chronicle of Old Florida and the Southwest* (New Haven: Yale University Press, 1921). Volume 23 in the Chronicles of America Series. Contains well-written accounts of exploration and colonization.

Corle, Edwin. *The Royal Highway (El Camino Real)* (Indianapolis: Bobbs-Merrill, 1949). A popular account up to the early 20th century.

Lummis, Charles F. *The Spanish Pioneers and the California Missions* (Chicago: A.C. McClurg & Co., 1931). A highly pro-Spanish account.

Moody, Ralph. *The Old Trails West* (New York: Crowell, 1963). A brief history of each of the main western trails; includes chapters on the Oregon and California trails, with excellent maps.

Riesenberg, Felix, Jr. *The Golden Road: The Story of California's Spanish Mission Trail* (New York: McGraw-Hill, 1962). Part of the American Trails Series. A popular account up through the 1950s.

Winther, Oscar Osburn. *Express and Stagecoach Days in California: From the Gold Rush to the Civil War* (Stanford University, California: Stanford University Press, 1936). A detailed account of the limited stagecoach period.

4

THE CAPE HORN ROUTE

> For five weeks I was beating and banging off that horrid place. It seems as though all the furies of the infernal region were let loose. Tremendous gales, snow and hail continuously, nights eighteen hours; sun nine degrees high and sometimes not see him for a week. A small vessel, all hands wet continually, and no chance to dry their clothes. Any person thinking there is pleasure in going to sea, I would advise them to double [round] Cape Horn.

That was Yankee Captain Francis A. Thompson's description of the passage round Cape Horn, the southernmost tip of South America. It would instantly be recognized by all the other sailors who ever made the voyage. With its icy waters, stormy winds, and dangerous currents, Cape Horn has always been one of the most difficult and dangerous trade routes in the world.

Yet despite its hazards, the Cape Horn Route played a major role in world history, at least for one short period. For several decades, the Cape Horn Route was the pathway of the Yankee ships that swept down the east coast of the Americas and up the west, on their way to the rich trade in East Asia.

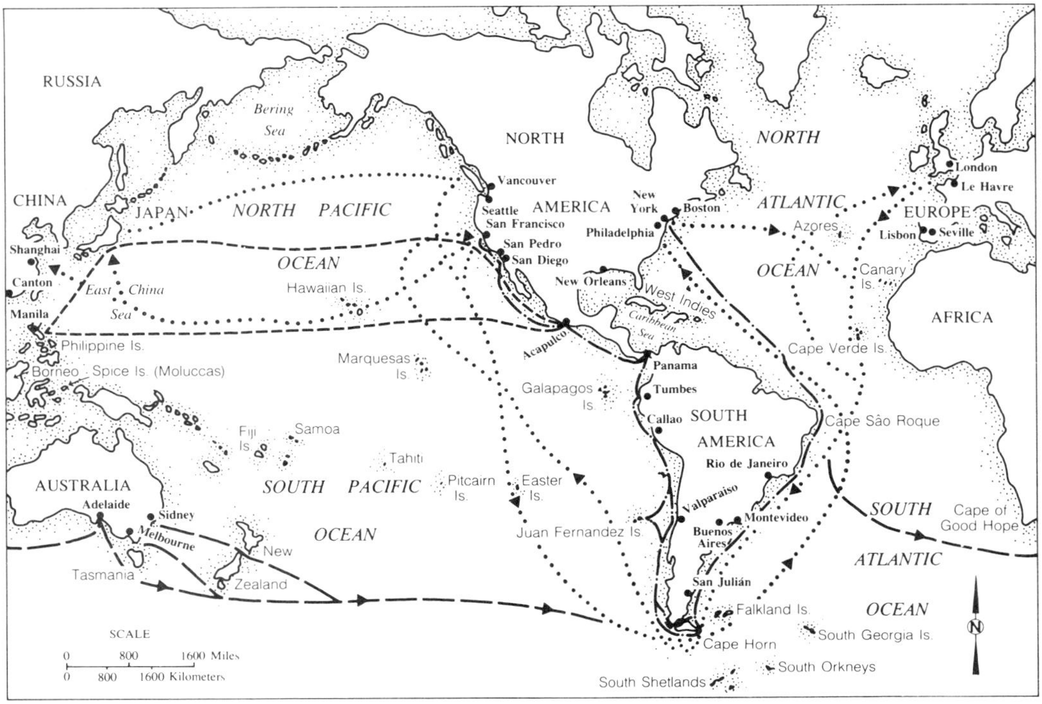

The Cape Horn Route

—·—·— Early Sailing Routes -------- Manila Galleon Route

·········· Late 19th Century Sailing Routes —— Round-the-World Route

This trade with China, India, and the Far East helped build the U.S. economy during the 19th century. And the connection between the Atlantic and the Pacific coasts was part of the process that led to the annexation of California, Oregon, and Hawaii, as well as the establishment of U.S. power in the Pacific.

The European Explorers

Searching for a Route to the East. The story of the Cape Horn route begins in the 15th and 16th centuries, as European explorers looked for a route to the Far East. For centuries, Europeans had enjoyed the rich gold, spices, silks, and ornaments that came from China, India, Southeast Asia, and the Spice Islands. At the same time, these goods could be found nowhere else in the world.

Yet the Europeans could not get these goods for themselves. They depended on Indian and Arab sailors who brought them from the Far East to the Middle East. From the Middle East, the goods could be brought to Europe. This process was expensive, and it was out of the Europeans' control. So in the 15th century, the Europeans began looking for their own routes to the Far East. One famous effort was the Spanish government's financing of Christopher Columbus. Columbus was looking for a route to China and India, but he landed in the Americas instead.

The Europeans soon realized that these continents offered riches of their own and began to exploit their resources. But they still wanted to get to the East. Many explorers continued to search for a way to sail *through* the Americas, hoping that somewhere there would be a sea passage that would take them the rest of the way around the globe. Explorers from Northern Europe searched for such a passage along the North American coast. Southern Europeans explored from the Caribbean southward.

Magellan Sets Out. The first European sailors to succeed in finding a route through the Americas was Ferdinand Magellan. Magellan was a Portuguese sailor who captained a fleet of old, worn-out Spanish ships. On September 20, 1519, Magellan set off for the South Atlantic.

Earlier explorers had already ruled out the part of South America that bulges out into the Atlantic (now part of the country of Brazil). They knew that this bulge could offer no sea passage to the Pacific. So Magellan explored farther down. He found the bay now called Rio de Janeiro, in modern-day Brazil, as well as Montevideo, in modern Uruguay.

South of the equator, the seasons are opposite to those north of the equator. So in late March of 1520, winter was just beginning in the south. Magellan decided to stop sailing for the winter and set up headquarters in the Bay of Port St. Julian, off southern Patagonia.

Magellan's decision was a poor one. This was the latitude known as the "Roaring Forties." It was called "roaring" because of the strong east winds. At this latitude, there are no huge masses of land to break the wind, so they blow very strongly, often at gale force.

Mutiny. Magellan's sailors became angry and dissatisfied with their difficult conditions. By the time winter had ended in August,

Magellan had to put down a mutiny among his crew. After the winter had ended, Magellan set out again. On October 21, 1520, the fleet came to a high cliff overlooking a strait (a narrow body of water, running between two pieces of land to connect two larger bodies of water). Today that cliff is called Cape Virgenes.

Magellan hoped that the strait would lead him from the Atlantic into the Pacific Ocean. The crew was skeptical. But Magellan insisted on exploring the strait For the next 31 days, that's what they did. A man named Antonio Pigafetta was on the voyage, and he describes their exploration like this:

> This strait is enclosed between lofty [high] mountains covered with snow, and it is likewise very deep, so that we were unable to anchor except quite close to shore, where was from 25 to 30 fathoms of water....
>
> At night came on a terrible hurricane, which lasted six and thirty hours, and forced us to quit our anchors and leave our vessels to the mercy of the winds and waves in the gulf.
>
> The two other vessels, equally buffeted [blown by the wind], were unable to double [round] a cape in order to rejoin us, so [the wind] drove them constantly toward what they conceived to be the bottom of a bay, they were apprehensive momentarily of being driven onshore. But at the instant they gave themselves up for lost, they saw a small opening, which they took for an inlet of the bay. Into this they entered, and perceiving that this channel was not closed, they threaded it, and found themselves in another, through which they pursued their course to another strait leading into a third bay still larger than the preceding.

At this point, those two other vessels decided to return and report to Magellan, who had almost given them up for lost. Then the whole fleet joined forces and continued the exploration—all except for one ship, which deserted, and sailed back to Spain with most of Magellan's supplies!

Meanwhile, the exploration of the strait continued. Another group of sailors was sent out. After several more days, reports Pigafetta:

> The sailors sent on this expedition returned, and announced their having seen the cape where the strait ended, and with it a great sea—that is to say, the ocean. We wept for joy. This cape

was...[named] Il Cape Deseado [the Desired Cape] for in truth we had long wished to see it.

Like most ships to follow, Magellan's ship, the *Victoria,* took a terrible beating rounding South America. (Authors' archives)

Scurvy. Although Magellan's crew had made a great discovery, the worst was not yet over. The crew understood that the world was round—but they thought that the world was much smaller than it actually is. Therefore, they expected Asia to be quite near. So they set off across the wide, unexplored Pacific Ocean. They had a lot of courage, but not very many supplies. Here is Pigafetta's description again:

> We sailed the space of three months and twenty days, without tasting any fresh provisions. The biscuit we were eating no longer deserved the name of bread; it was nothing but dust, and worms which had consumed the substance; and what is more, it smelled intolerably, being impregnated with the urine of mice. The water we were obliged to drink was equally putrid [rotting] and offensive.
>
> We were even so far reduced, that we might not die of hunger, to eat pieces of the leather with which the mainyard [a pole that supports a sail] was covered...constantly exposed to the water, sun, and wind, [these pieces] were so hard that they required being soaked four or five days in the sea in order to render them supple [bendable]; after this we broiled them to eat. Frequently indeed we were obliged to subsist on sawdust,

> and even mice, a food so disgusting, were sought after with such avidity that they sold for half a ducat apiece.

Magellan's men were not only starving. They were also suffering from a terrible disease called scurvy, which comes from not getting enough vitamin C. Since Magellan's men were eating no fresh fruits or vegetables, they were not getting any vitamin C at all. The disease ran a terrible course

> in which the gums swelled as to hide the teeth...whence those affected were thus incapable of chewing their food....Besides those [19] who died, we had from 25 to 30 sailors ill, who suffered dreadful pains in their arms, legs, and other parts of the body.

Still amazingly, most of the sailors survived—and were the first people that we know of to cross the Pacific Ocean. Eventually, they landed on some desert islands, where they found some food and water. Later they arrived at a group of islands that they named the Philippines, after Spain's King Philip II.

Spain and the New Route. Magellan himself was killed by some local people in the Philippines. But the rest of the sailors in his crew tried to return to Spain. As it happened, only one ship made it. Of the five ships that had started out, only one actually sailed all the way around the world. Even so, just that one ship's load of spices from Southeast Asia more than paid for the great cost of sending out Magellan's whole fleet! More important still, Magellan had opened up a new sea route that the Europeans could profitably use to reach the Asian markets.

Spain tried to make this trading route profitable as soon as possible. In 1525, they sent another fleet of seven ships to the strait that Magellan had explored, named the Strait of Magellan in his honor. This second fleet hit even rougher weather than Magellan had come across. Many people were killed by the strong winds and stormy weather, including four fleet commanders. Many sailors deserted. Only three of the seven ships passed through the Strait of Magellan, and only one ship reached the Philippines.

Spain continued to send other fleets along this difficult course, as well as to the continent of South America. But the southernmost route was rarely used in the 16th century. It was too dangerous and too difficult. The Spanish preferred to sail to Mexico or Panama, break their ships apart, and carry them over land to reach the Pacific (see Chapter 1). Then they would reconstruct their ships on the west coast and sail on.

The British Pirate-Explorers

Francis Drake. The next group that came to explore the Cape Horn Route was the British. In the 1570s, British explorer Francis Drake sailed into the southern world. Like the other European explorers of the time, Drake was seeking new routes through the Americas to the East. Like Magellan before him, Drake passed through the Strait of Magellan. But the winds blowing off the Pacific Ocean drove him south, where he made an interesting discovery.

When Magellan had passed through, he had seen land to the south. He named that land *Tierra del Fuego*, the "Land of Fire," because he had seen many fires burning in the hills. Magellan and the other Europeans of his time believed that Tierra del Fuego was part of yet another southern continent. But as Francis Drake discovered, Magellan was wrong. Tierra del Fuego was not a huge

Cape Horn sailors found Tierra del Fuego ("Land of Fire") a peculiar name for this land of ice and desolation. (National Maritime Museum)

continent, but a small group of islands. After Drake made his voyage, Europeans had to redraw their maps.

After rounding Cape Horn he traveled up the west coast of South America. There he attacked Spanish colonial ships and settlements as he worked his way north. He was looking for their money and their goods—but he also wanted their maps. Drake wanted to pass on to the English all the Spanish knowledge of this part of the world.

Eventually, Drake made his way up past San Francisco, beyond Spanish territory of the time. He claimed the region for England and called it *Nova Albion*, Latin for "New England." Then he continued on across the Pacific, using the Spanish maps he had taken.

Thomas Cavendish. The British continued to send pirate-explorers to South America. Another such man, Thomas Cavendish, left a description of his adventures. From his own story, he seems to have been a vicious fighter indeed:

> I navigated along the coast of Chili [sic], Peru and Nueva Espanna [New Spain, the modern country of Mexico], where I made great spoiles; I burnt and sunk nine sailes of ships small and great. All the villages and townes that ever I landed at, I burnt and spoiled.

But later, most pirate voyages were failures. Many men died and many ships were lost, with very little result.

Cape Horn

The Dutch. The Dutch, too, sent ships through the Strait of Magellan. Like the other Europeans of the time, they wanted the gold and silver that could be found in Peru, Mexico, and Bolivia. Dutch exploration proved to be very valuable to other Europeans, for it was two Dutchmen who first found the way around Cape Horn.

The Dutch built on Drake's discovery that there was no continent south of the Strait of Magellan. In 1615 Jacob Le Maire and William Schouten led an expedition down the east coast of South America, past the Strait of Magellan and around the southern tip of the continent. They named the tip of South America "Hoorn," after Schouten's home town in Holland (later the name was changed to Horn).

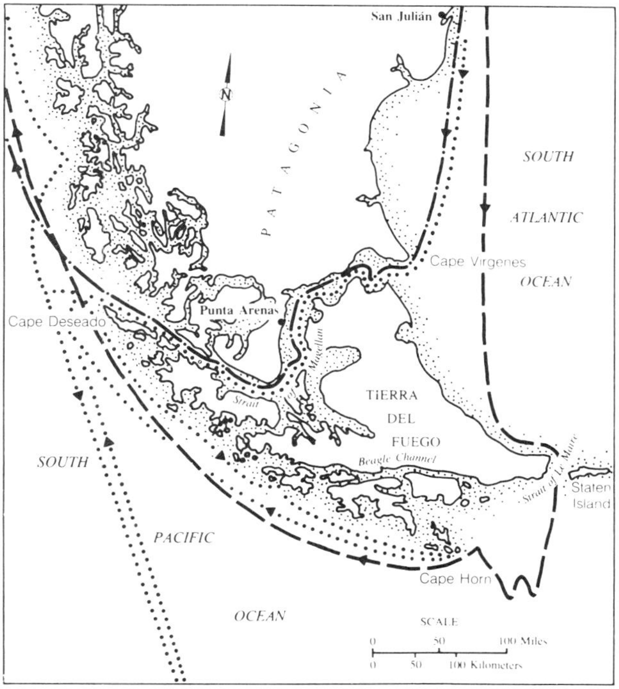

Cape Horn

—·—·— Magellan's Route

— — — Le Maire's Route

··········· Drake's Route

The seas off Cape Horn are very stormy because it is here that the waters mix from three oceans: the Atlantic, the Pacific, and the Antarctic. Both the Dutch and the Spanish tried to use the Cape Horn route to sail east. But neither group could. The weather in the area continued to beleaguer ships and sailors. By the middle of the 17th century, the Dutch abandoned Cape Horn and decided to use the Cape of Good Hope Route around Africa instead.

The Spanish. The Spanish were not really upset about the difficulty of the Cape Horn Route. So far, they were the only European nation to have colonies in South America. The harder it was for other nations to sail in the area, the more they would leave Spain's west coast colonies alone.

Spain had made a law that no one could trade with any of the Spanish colonies except for a few cities the Spanish had designated. They used the law to strictly control all trade so that they could charge high taxes and make more money. But other European countries were eager to expand their trade. They traded illegally with Spanish ports in the Caribbean and the South Atlantic. In fact, the great port of Buenos Aires was developed mainly by Europeans who were conducting illegal trade with Spanish colonials.

Europe was involved in many wars during the 17th century, which was another reason that the Cape Horn Route stayed unused for a long time.

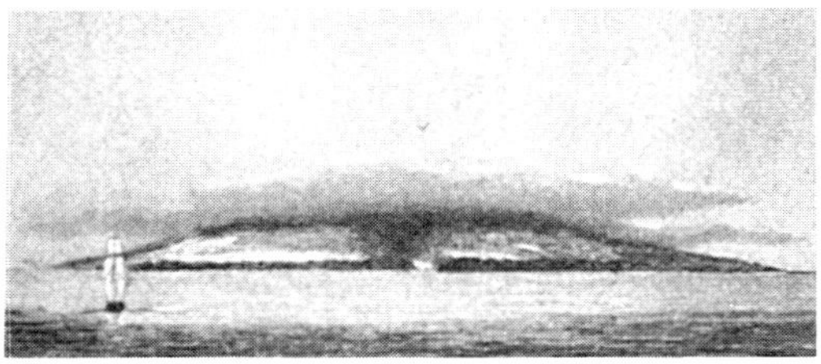

Ships sailing on the Cape Horn Route welcomed island resting places off South America's west coast, like the Galapagos Islands, shown here in four views. (From Fitzroy and Darwin, *Narrative ... of the Beagle*, London, 1839)

New Explorers. But in the second half of the 17th century, Europe became relatively peaceful, and explorers began to come back to the Cape Horn Route, moving through Tierra del Fuego, the South Georgia Islands, and other islands around the southern tip of South America. They filled in many details about these islands, where they were located, and how they were shaped. Maps of this part of the world were becoming more accurate.

The Three Voyages of Captain Cook. But the most important explorations in this part of the world took place in the late 18th century. The English sailor and explorer, Captain Cook, made three

This is Rio de Janeiro, Brazil, as it appeared to Charles Darwin, when he was exploring along the Cape Horn Route. (From Fitzroy and Darwin, *Narrative ... of the Beagle*, London, 1839)

voyages around the world, with many exciting discoveries in the Pacific. Cook's discoveries pointed the way to new opportunities for trade. On his last Pacific voyage, he took some sea-otter pelts from the northwest coast of North America. After he died, his crew traded them to merchants in Asia. The sea-otter pelts had been "bought" from Native Americans for a few trinkets. But they were sold in China for a huge profit.

When the British learned about this, they realized how potentially profitable it would be to travel between the Americas and Asia. They quickly moved to develop the Cape Horn Route, and were soon joined by the U.S. merchants in New England.

Around the Horn to China

The China Trade. When the British and U.S. merchants realized how profitable the China trade was, they made it a major focus of their activity. They stripped the islands and coasts of the Atlantic and the Pacific of any products that might possibly interest China. The Chinese were interested in very little from the outside world. But Europe and the United States prized Chinese products: tea, medicines, silk, fine porcelain "china." To get these products, they had to find something that the Chinese wanted in exchange.

At first, the main items from the West that the Chinese were prepared to trade for were sea-otter fur and ginseng. Ginseng was a special root, used in making medicines. It grew only in Manchuria (northeastern China) and parts of the Americas.

The Cape Horn Route Grows. In the early years of the China trade, the ships that left North America in the spring took the Cape of Good Hope Route, around Africa. The winds were favorable in this direction, and ships did not have to risk the bitter winter weather of Cape Horn. But U.S. ships leaving late in the year—near the southern summertime—usually took the Cape Horn Route.

Over the years, however, the Cape Horn Route came to be chosen by most of the U.S. ships, no matter what the time of year. That way, they could pick up their trade goods—especially fur from northwestern America—on the way.

Yankee Traders

United States Expansion. At first the Europeans had the advantage in the China trade, because they had more products to sell than the people in the United States. The United States was still a new country in the 18th century and did not have the long traditions of craft work and manufacturing that Europe had.

Then, in 1789, the French rose up to overthrow their king, and all Europe fell into political turmoil, significantly disrupting Europe's trade with China for several decades. The United States moved quickly to take up the slack. Yankee traders collected sea-otter pelts from the Oregon coast and Pacific Ocean islands to barter with China. Their trade added up to about $500,000 per year.

Later, as the sea-otter population dwindled, the pelts became more scarce. At the same time, the Native Americans who traded them began asking for more money and goods in exchange for the precious pelts.

So the Yankee traders went to look for other products to trade. They began to hunt the seals of the South Atlantic to sell their pelts. They sailed around the Malvinas Islands, Tierra del Fuego, and even further south, looking for seals. In 1820 a sealing ship discovered Antarctica, the southern continent that includes the South Pole.

The Pacific supplied other products for the China trade: sandalwood, birds' nests (from which the Chinese made soup), beche-de-mer (foot-long edible sea slugs), coral moss (also used as food), and mother-of-pearl. These products were found on the Hawaiian Islands, Fiji, the Marquesas, and elsewhere. Eventually, this trade became the basis for the United States taking control of many of these islands.

The Yankees and California. In the same way, Yankee traders opened up California. At this time, California was a Spanish colony. Most Spanish colonies were forbidden to trade with anyone on their own. But California was cut off from direct contact with Spain and mostly ignored by the Spanish colonial government in Mexico. California was even more cut off between 1810 and 1821, when Mexico was fighting for independence.

At the same time, the Europeans living in California were badly in need of more goods. They were happy to trade for New England goods. In exchange, they traded their cattle products—hides and tallow (a kind of fat used in making soap and candles).

Whaling Days

Pacific Whaling Begins. Yankees found another source of wealth in the Pacific—whales. These magnificent animals provided valuable oil used in the lamps of the time, as well as ivory, whalebone, ambergris (used in making perfume), and other important products.

New England whalers had been working in the North Atlantic for a long time. During the 18th century, they had moved across the Atlantic to the Cape Verde Islands off Africa, and also into the South Atlantic. But during the American Revolution, whaling had stopped; the ships were needed to fight the war. The war destroyed so many ships that only a few were left after it was over. Many Yankee whalers had to sail on British ships out of Canada or French ships out of Dunkirk.

It was a group of New England sailors using a British ship that sailed around Cape Horn in 1787, looking for the whales of the Pacific. This journey marked the beginning Pacific whaling.

Dangers and Hardships. By the mid-19th century, New England whalers were working off Japan and even beyond the North Pacific, into the Bering Sea. These whalers often took dangerous chances. In the 1870s, some whaling ships stayed in these northern

Arctic waters so late into the winter that they were trapped in the ice and crushed.

Yankee trading activity required a good deal of land-based support. Ships leaving the North Atlantic needed to stop on the way to get supplies and make repairs. They often called in at Rio de Janeiro, the Cape Verde Islands, and the Malvinas.

Then it was time to face the Horn's east winds, which were so strong that they led to the nickname "Old Cape Stiff." Ships also faced the storms and whirling currents produced by the meeting of the three oceans. The writer Richard Henry Dana, Jr., in his book *Two Years Before the Mast,* described the sudden change from a fine sunny day on the South Atlantic. He uses lots of technical shipboard language, but his meaning is clear:

> Hurrying upon deck, we found a large black cloud rolling on toward us from the south-west, and blackening the whole heavens. "Here comes Cape Horn!" said the chief mate; and we had hardly time to haul down and clew up, before it was upon us. In a few moments, a heavier sea was raised than I had ever seen before and...the little brig [whaler], which was no better than a bathing machine, plunged into it, and all the forward part of her was under water; the sea pouring in through the bow-ports and hawse-hole and over the knight-heads, threatening to wash everything overboard. In the lee scuppers it was up to a man's waist. We sprang aloft and double reefed the topsails, and furied all the other sails, and made all snug. But this would not do; the brig was laboring and straining against the head sea, and the gale was growing worse and worse. At the same time sleet and hail were driving with all fury against us.

The Cape had more dangers still. Huge icebergs floated in the Antarctic waters, sometimes rising out of the water like ghost ships. Many crews were shipwrecked by these mountains of ice.

Rest Stops. Many ships did not survive all these dangers. Those that did desperately needed to stop somewhere for rest and repairs. One place was Juan Fernandez Island. Dana described it as rising "like a deep blue cloud out of the sea" off the coast of Chile. There were other rest stops along the South American Coast, in the

The island of Juan Fernandez was a prime anchorage for resting the crew, repairing the ship, and taking on water. (By Richard Walter, from George Anson, Esq., *A Voyage round the World ...*, London, 1748)

modern countries of Chile and Peru. Farther out in the ocean, Honolulu, Hawaii, became the prime port for rest and repair.

The ships that were trading hides and tallows stopped in San Francisco, San Diego, and San Pedro, which was later renamed Los Angeles. But many ships did not like to stop in California, because the captains feared that their crews would desert their ships and stay on to make their homes there. This phenomenon was called "leaving their consciences at Cape Horn."

An American Sea

The Rise of the United States. In the 17th and 18th centuries, the Pacific Ocean had been nicknamed "The Spanish Sea." That was because the Spanish had the greatest presence there.

But in the 19th century, the Pacific was fast becoming the "American Sea." The trend was speeded up in 1815, after Spain stopped its trade with the Philippines.

Britain was still an important power, however. British whalers worked in the Pacific. Sometimes they attacked American ships when the two countries were at war. Sometimes, too, French pirates attacked the Americans.

The President finally called out the U.S. Navy to protect U.S. interests. During the War of 1812, a ship was sent to the Pacific to clear British whalers from the area. This was a serious blow to

British whaling. Later, the U.S. Navy set up a base at Valparaiso, Chile. From there, ships patrolled the Pacific.

The Spread of U.S. Influence. The United States affected South America in many ways. As we have seen, it brought U.S. military power into the area. But it also brought ideas about independence and democracy, which affected South American independence movements. American missionaries also traveled to Pacific islands.

During the 19th century, the United States expanded its influence in North America as well. Gradually, it took over the land between the eastern colonies and California. After the Mexican War of 1846, it took California, along with much of the American Southwest. In the same period, it took much of the northern Pacific coast. This expansion continued to increase U.S. influence in the Pacific.

Before the discovery of gold, San Francisco was a very modest village indeed. (California Historical Society)

Gold Is Found. In January, 1848, gold was discovered in California. This simple fact was to change history for both California and the Cape Horn Route. The effect on California was to draw hundreds of thousands of people to the gold fields and to the businesses that served them. The effect on the Cape Horn Route was to make it far more popular, for it was one of the key routes for traveling west.

By the end of 1849, over 300 ships of all sizes and descriptions were anchored at San Francisco harbor. Many of them had traveled from the East around Cape Horn.

For most of these ships, it was a one-way trip since all of the people they brought wanted to remain in California. Some of them were used on the rivers of California. Others became floating homes, stores, or prisons. Still others were broken up for wood that could be used to build on land. Some of the ships in San Francisco's harbor were simply left to rot and sink in the harbor. Many more burned in the great harbor fire of 1851.

Regular trading or whaling ships did not like to stop at San Francisco—their crews wanted to desert and look for gold! Some ships even kept their men under lock and key while they were in gold-country ports.

On the way to California, these gold-seekers—on an easy part of the voyage—take advantage of some fair weather on the deck of their clipper. (The Mariners Museum, Newport News, Virginia)

Clipper Ships. The flow of west-bound ships caused a crisis on the East Coast. There were not enough ships for regular shipping, and not enough crews to sail them. New ships had to be built and men had to be found.

Many of these new ships were the famous clipper ships. The clippers were the fastest ships of their day by the 1850s. The trip between Boston and San Francisco generally took six to seven months, or 200 days, although the older ships took much longer. As new sailing methods evolved, the time was eventually cut to about 90 days. The graceful clipper ships with their high masts became the mainstay for the Cape Horn trip to China.

New Pacific Markets. With their fine new ships and improved sailing methods, Yankee traders were able to take advantage of new markets in the Pacific. Many West Coast cities were short of basic goods because their workers had left for the gold fields.

The gold miners wanted to buy goods with their new riches, as well. For both reasons, most goods brought around the Horn to California were sold before they were ever unloaded. People would row out to trading ships that were anchored off the California coast and pay huge prices for whatever was aboard. Even though many prospectors (people looking for gold) died poor, all the traders on the Cape Horn Route made their fortunes.

After the discovery of gold in California, a forest of ships crowded San Francisco's harbor. (Lithograph by W. Roosen after a drawing by Capt. Collinson, National Maritime Museum)

Traders made profits out of some unlikely things. Some brought ice packed in sawdust from New England. It traveled around Cape Horn to steamy Panama City and other Pacific ports. A German immigrant named Levi Strauss sold pants: he devised new work pants made out of canvas, a cloth from the French town of Nîmes. This cloth, "de Nîmes," became famous as the material for Levis denim pants—the first blue jeans.

The U.S. west coast wasn't the only place where traders could make fortunes. In the middle of the 19th century, Europeans and Americans forced China and Japan to begin trading again with foreigners. This made the Cape Horn Route even more important.

Days of Decline

Railroads. But even in these years of success, the heyday of the Cape Horn Route was passing. In 1855 the Panama Railroad was finished. Suddenly, traders could sail to the east coast of Panama, transport their goods across the country by rail, and pick up new ships on the west coast. Passengers could travel in the same way. This cut thousands of miles off the Cape Horn Route, which cost that route much prime freight business.

In a few more years, in 1869, a railroad was finally built across the United States. Now goods could be shipped from the U.S. east coast directly overland to the west coast. Railroads would take more and more business away from the Cape Horn Route.

The Civil War. Shipping was upset even more during the U.S. Civil War of the 1860s. Most Pacific ships were taken for war use. Confederate cruisers destroyed several trading ships that were going round the Horn, as well as many ships in the Pacific. After the war, the whaling industry fell into decline. In 1859 U.S. oil wells began producing their own oil, which meant that whaling was no longer so necessary.

Pacific trade in general became less important after the Civil War. By then it had to compete with the American West. The riches of China and the Pacific now seemed much less desirable when compared with the ranches of California, and the free, open land of the West. In earlier years, people seeking a fortune might go to sea. Now they went west.

Ships on the Cape Horn Route therefore had trouble finding and keeping experienced crews. Crews had also heard discouraging stories about the Cape Horn voyage. Here is another description of that difficult voyage from the 1840 book by Richard Henry Dana, Jr., *Two Years Before the Mast*:

> We had now got hardened to the Cape weather....Our clothes were all wet through, and the only change was from wet to more wet. It was in vain to think of reading or working below, for we were too tired, the hatchways were closed down, and everything was wet and uncomfortable, black and dirty, heaving and pitching. We had only to come below when the watch was out, wring out our wet clothes, hang them up, and turn in and sleep as soundly as we could until the watch was called again.

This American clipper ship, the *Comet*, is caught in a hurricane off Bermuda. (The Mariners Museum, Newport News, Virginia)

These conditions were bad enough. But Dana wrote that the sailors were also treated very badly by the captain, which made things even worse:

> The captain stood on the...deck, a few feet from [the man in irons], and a little raised, so as to have a good swing at him....A man—a human being, made in God's likeness—fastened up and flogged like a beast!...The first and almost uncontrollable impulse was resistance....But...what is there for sailors to do? If they resist, it is mutiny; and if they succeed, and take the vessel, it is piracy.

Mutiny is when sailors revolt and try to take over a ship. There were very strict laws against mutiny, in order to protect captains from disaffected crews like the ones Dana described. Eventually, descriptions like Dana's brought about changes. Sailors were no longer treated so badly. But by then, the Cape Horn Route had declined.

Bulky Freight Around the Horn. The Horn continued to be a major route for the kinds of bulky freight that did not travel well by railroad. Guano—bird droppings used for manure—and grain were two important products that were shipped by sea. Clipper ships were designed for speed, not bulk. So as bulky freight became more important, clippers were replaced by roomier ships. Eventually, steamships took over from sailing ships of all kinds.

Modern Times

Steamships. As steamships took over the Cape Horn Route, they also changed it slightly. Steamships were not so much at the mercy of winds and currents, so they were able to brave the difficult Strait of Magellan. Although sailboats had avoided the Strait, steamships sailed through it.

By the turn of the 20th century, steamers were bringing California wine and Hawaiian sugar to the East, and the New York–San Francisco trip was down to 60 days. But railroads were faster and commercial shipping was done by sea only when there was no other way.

However, the Cape Horn Route was important for military reasons. It was the route used to reach the Pacific territories, including the Hawaiian Islands and the Philippines. These territories were an important part of U.S. expansion to the east.

Finally, in 1914, the Panama Canal was opened. Now sea travel could pass far more quickly between east and west, taking the short cut through Panama rather than the long way round the cape.

The Cape Horn Route's Uses. The Cape Horn Route continues to be useful in the present day, however. The Panama Canal works by using *locks*, narrow pools of water that can be filled and emptied, floating ships up and down to help them pass through the canal. These locks have been widened several times throughout the 20th century, but ships continue to grow in width. Some ships are too large for the Panama Canal, such as some aircraft carriers, cargo ships, and supertankers. They must find other routes, including the Cape of Good Hope and the Cape Horn Route.

The Cape Horn Route was also useful during wartime. British and German ships fought nearby in both World Wars I and II. German ships in the South Atlantic tried to cut off food supplies to the Allies brought in from Argentina, Australia, and New Zealand. But the Allies fought to keep these supplies coming in.

Nevertheless, the heyday of the Cape Horn Route is now over. The few surviving Cape Horn sailors see themselves as the last of a dying breed. Here is a poem by Harry Kemp, written in the 1940s, where he remembers the great days that are past:

I am eighty years old and somewhat
But I give to God the praise
That they made a sailor of me
In the good old clipper days....
You could spy our great ships running
White-clouded, tier on tier,
You could hear their tramping thunder
As they leaned-to racing near;
And it was "Heigh-ho and ho, my lad,"
When we were outward bound,
And we sang full many a chanty
As we walked the capstan round.
Aye, we sang full many a chanty
As we drove through wind and wet,
To the music of five oceans
That rings in memory yet.

Go, drive your dirty freighters
That fill the sky with reek—
But we—we took in skysails
high as a mountain peak...

Suggestions for Further Reading

Dodge, Ernest S. *New England and the South Seas* (Cambridge, Mass.: Harvard University Press, 1965). Focuses on their mutual influences.

Greenbie, Sydney, and Marjorie Greenbie. *Gold of Ophir; or the Lure that Made America* (Garden City, New York: Doubleday, Page, 1925). On how the idea of the East helped open both sea and land routes.

Hough, Richard. *The Blind Horn's Hate* (New York: Norton, 1971). A sea-lover's history of the southern tip of South America.

Morison, Samuel Eliot. *The European Discovery of America: The Southern Voyages A.D. 1492–1616* (New York: Oxford University Press, 1974). A closely detailed account of the earliest explorations.

Penrose, Boies. *Travel and Discovery in the Renaissance, 1430–1620* (New York: Atheneum, 1965; reprint of the 1952 Harvard University Press edition). An excellent work; two chapters focus on discoveries along the Cape Horn Route.

Rydell, Raymond A. *Cape Horn to the Pacific: The Rise and Decline of an Ocean Highway* (Berkeley and Los Angeles: University of California Press, 1952). A prime work on the Cape Horn Route.

Tamarin, Alfred, and Shirley Glubok. *Voyaging to Cathay: Americans in the China Trade* (New York: Viking, 1976). A well-illustrated book on Yankees in the China trade.

Villiers, Alan. *The War With Cape Horn* (New York: Scribner's, 1971). A personal account of the great days of sailing ships on Cape Horn.

INDEX

Italic numbers indicate illustrations

C